4/19

The Quest

Chris,
Thanks for being a big part of a special team!
Coach Will

The Quest

On the Path to Knowledge and Wisdom

WILL FREEMAN

FORWARD BY U.S. OLYMPIC COACH
DR. JOE VIGIL

Copyright 2009 Will Freeman

All rights reserved. No part of this book may be used or reproduced in any manner without the written permission of the author. Printed in the United States of America.

ISBN: 149593232X
ISBN 13: 9781495932328
Library of Congress Control Number: 2014903300
CreateSpace Independent Publishing Platform
North Charleston, South Carolina

For Evelyn, Cameron, Deidre, and Nicolette.
Without the love and support of my family,
I could not have written this.

The privilege of a lifetime is being who you are.
                                    Joseph Campbell

When you were born, you cried and the world rejoiced.
Live your life so that when you die, the world cries and
you rejoice.
                                    White Elk

Preface

There are times when our life experiences illuminate truths to us. Sometimes the power of these moments can change the way we view our path, if not alter it completely. If we recognize it and heed its call, intuition often inspires these moments. This special story unfolded after one of those occasions. It would result in a personal odyssey that would change both the way I view my life and the way I teach and mentor others.

The amazing events chronicled in this book occurred over a ten-year period. It's a story about father-child relationships, Native American philosophy, spirituality, mentoring, and motorcycles. Mostly, it's about self-growth and the results of the choices we make in life.

I carried my trusted old leather journal with me on my journey, and I'm glad I did. I recorded the events as they happened. If I hadn't, I'm not sure I would have believed it all.

By all accounts, I've lived a fortunate life. I grew up in Lexington, Kentucky, the second of five boys in a middle-class family of solid values. My dad was a cop. It was a demanding job, but one he enjoyed, and he was good at it. By the time I had graduated high school, Dad was a police chief. My mom was a full-time mother raising five boys through the 1950's and '60's. Of the two, hers was the harder job. She too, was good at it.

Having picked the right parents, I was fortunate to have a genetic gift that allowed me to attend the University of Florida on an athletic scholarship. I had a wonderful experience there. Two degrees later, my athletic days over, I found a job at Grinnell College, where I was hired to coach Track & Field, and later, Cross Country. I've been teaching and coaching at Grinnell for twenty-nine years. It's the only job I've ever had.

I met and married a very special woman, and we have three wonderful kids. By all accounts, I've been truly blessed.

As good as my life looked on the surface, something was missing, and I knew it. Like many, I've long been on a personal spiritual search to find meaning in my life. Over the years, I've read many, many books on all forms of spiritual enlightenment and experienced many different religions. The books and the religious experiences have given me knowledge, but not the wisdom and spirituality I wanted. Then things began to happen in my life that would change everything. This is that story.

WAF

Forward

In every age there is someone, a special person, who stands out from the rest of the field. Someone who stands out because of the philosophy they have developed in their jobs, in their interaction with colleagues, their teams, their families, and friends. One whose lifestyle is practicing the pursuit of excellence in every one of the mini-environments they live. That person is Will Freeman. The ten-year experience he so beautifully portrays in "The Quest" illustrates how he has developed a philosophy of life that he both lives and teaches.

In this day and age we live in a culture of narcissism and the quest for money, power, and materialism. It's a culture where those who don't win are often viewed as failures. Will Freeman has eloquently portrayed, with the help of a very special mentor, how to live one's life with purpose and meaning. He teaches that there can be no excellence without right living, and adheres to the principle of unending improvement as what is most important. He shows that if the focus is on a healthy process, the end result takes care of itself.

I have known Will Freeman for a period of 25 years and have seen him practice the tenets in "The Quest". I have been on clinic panels and in leadership positions with him and have seen his convictions come out loud and clear. He is a true teacher. As I travel nationally and internationally presenting coaching clinics, I have seen a great need for what he portrays in teaching people "how to live", rather than "how to make a living".

As a fellow educator and coach, I would be the first to recommend this book as required reading for all teachers, coaches, parents and professional leaders. I read it three times! As a 50-year professional in the field of education and sport, I have taken a look at my own life and seen where I could have been much better has I followed the philosophy so eloquently portrayed in the book. I believe "The Quest" is a must read.

Dr. Joe I. Vigil
U.S. Olympic Distance Coach 1988-2008
National and International Coaching Educator
USATF, USOC, IAAF

Part One

The Big Adventure

Our first teacher is our own heart.
                                   Cheyenne Saying

*I*n the spring of 1999, I was finishing my eighteenth year of collegiate coaching when my son and I began planning a special summer trip. I knew in advance that this vacation held something special in store for us. It was going to be a father-son trip, a chance to spend some much-needed quality time together. The trip would not include my wife Evelyn and our two young girls, Deidre and Nicolette. They were off to Holland with Evelyn's mom for a three-week "girls-only" trip to where "Oma" grew up. My twelve-year-old son Cameron and I would be on our own for at least three weeks, and we planned to make the most of it.

As the trip approached, I heard Harry Chapin's haunting ballad "Cat's in the Cradle" several times on the radio, no doubt part of a repeating playlist. Each time I heard it, I was drawn to the words. I knew the song well, feeling both the truth and pain in the lyrics. It's about how our children grow up to be just like us, driven by everyday motivations that keep us from being the parents our kids deserve. Wishing that I'd been closer to my dad when I was young, I didn't want my son to grow up without knowing me. I was intent on spending some quality time with him while I still had a chance. He was already twelve ... with only six more years until he would leave home for college. I knew that those years would be critical to his development as he began to define his place in the world. I also knew that I wasn't giving him the time I should. The summer break provided the perfect time for us to have a rare get-away together. What would make this trip extra special was the mode of transportation -- a motorcycle.

I'd grown up with motorcycles and knew that it was the only way to make this kind of trip. On a bike, you're immersed in the environment with all your senses: the feel of air on skin, the smells in the air and the unmuted sights of the road. In a car, you're isolated in a cocoon, apart from the world around you. I wanted Cameron to experience the trip at the deepest level, and I knew that going on a bike would provide a very special memory. After months of researching motorcycles and weighing all the variables of the trip, we chose a big six-cylinder Honda Valkyrie cruiser with luggage bags and a big touring windshield. It had more than enough power to carry us, and our gear, up the steepest mountains.

A great part of the fun was planning our route. Since it was Cameron's trip, I wanted him to plot our destinations. He was intent on seeing California, especially seeing Universal Studios and Disneyland. While this destination was not especially appealing to me, I would honor his wishes. It was his trip and I was just happy that we would later ride up the Pacific Coast Highway to Oregon and Washington.

The Big Adventure

Having read *Zen and the Art of Motorcycle Maintenance* a couple of times over the years, I was moved by Robert Pirsig's father-son motorcycle trip across the country in 1968 and his search for quality and meaning in his life. I yearned for such a trip with my son in search of answers to questions that all men face ... some, later than others. I felt Cameron, at twelve years old, was ready for such a trip. At forty-four, I knew I was.

In the end, we wouldn't see Oregon or Washington. Nor would I have to face the challenges of Los Angeles traffic on a motorcycle. Our ultimate course ended up being the antithesis of the original Hollywood goal. The trip would become something very different than what we had planned... and it would change both of us.

THE JOURNEY BEGINS

With its gloss black paint and polished chrome (so bright we could barely look at it without sunglasses), the big six-cylinder bike had a commanding presence. We had to laugh when we donned our black full-face helmets and black riding jackets and looked in the mirror. Cameron commented,

"Dad, we look like Darth Vader and son." He was right ... we were an imposing pair.

We took several days to pack for the trip, making sure we laid out everything we might need for the three weeks ahead; rain gear, clothing for different conditions, lots of camping gear, maps, and of course, my trusty journal. I'm sure we were carrying more than we needed, but the bike was capable of handling the load. We were prepared for most anything we might face.

After rain delayed our start, we finally left Grinnell just after noon on July 5th. A short stop at the Honda dealer in Des Moines to put on a thumb-activated cruise control, and we were off for real. We gassed up, and pointed the bike west on I-80, both of us giddy with excitement about the trip ahead. I'd been reading up on beautiful drives in each of the states we would pass through. I wanted Cameron to see the beauty of the country in a way that we couldn't if trapped in a car. Like life itself, the journey was the focus of this trip, not the destination.

With hard saddlebags packed with clothing and an extra bag of our camping gear strapped to the luggage rack behind us, we were finally off on what Cameron called "the big adventure." It would become that, and much more, before it was over.

We had hoped to make Kearney, Nebraska before nightfall. While gassing up two hours short of Kearney, I struck up a conversation with a man traveling east. He stepped out from behind the gas pump and said,

"Beautiful bike! Man, that thing is huge! Looks like you guys are off on a big trip."

I smiled, adding to the small talk,

"Yep, we're headed west."

His smile left his face as he responded,

"I just came from west of here. You're about to hit some really bad weather ahead -- tornadoes and high winds -- you might want to start looking for a place to park that thing."

I thanked him as we mounted up, feeling a bit uncomfortable about the potential bad weather. We had rainproof

The Big Adventure

gear, but nothing for fighting tornadoes. I could see a cloud line ahead that hinted of a big front moving in, and I knew we would likely ride into it within the hour.

We were smart to stop. There were no tornadoes, but fierce winds and driving rain that forced cars and trucks off the highway. We found a motel room for the night, choosing not to test our toughness on day one. I'm glad ... we might not have recovered from it.

As I pulled down the covers on my bed, thinking about the trip ahead, I noticed Cameron's journal open on his bed as he slept. There was only one short entry: "First day over, butt is numb."

We awoke the next morning to great weather, clear and cool, and continued west toward the mountains of Colorado. The mountains had always felt like a spiritual magnet for me, and my young family had taken several vacations in Colorado. Unable to fully explain it, I just felt better when in the mountains. "A little bit closer to God," I would explain to others. I doubt they understood. I'm not sure I did either.

A gas stop and a promised go-cart ride in North Platte Nebraska gave us a break from the saddle. As I watched Cameron ride the carts twice, I reflected on how big he was getting. Mature in some ways, yet with so much to learn in other ways, I knew he was a lot like me: a bit of a rebel, very competitive and a free thinker. 'Who will he turn out to be,' I wondered as I watched him turn lap after lap.

"Dad, I'm a pro at this! Did you see me drive by those guys?" he asked after his final ride.

"I sure did, Cam. Those poor souls never had a chance," I responded with a smile, giving him the answer I knew he wanted. "I also saw that they warned you about driving a little too hard. You almost forced that one kid off the track." I said it with a smile, making sure he knew that I'd seen the incident.

He returned the smile, saying confidently,

"He got in my way, Dad."

I laughed, and made a mental note that we'd have to talk sometime about our inherent need to compare ourselves to others. Sensing it was too early on the trip to take on a topic like competition, we mounted up and continued west to Denver. It was a dry and desolate ride as we made a slow climb in altitude toward the Rocky Mountains.

Arriving in the Mile High City at 7:00 p.m., we caught the last of rush hour traffic as we made our way to the suburb of Cherry Creek, the home of my favorite bookstore, The Tattered Cover. After finding a room, we had a dinner of Mexican food and walked to a nearby cinema to see a film. There were plenty to choose from at the big multiplex. For some reason, it was Robert Redford's <u>The Horse Whisperer</u> that spoke to both of us. I bought two tickets and some popcorn; and, we settled into a couple of seats in the middle of the huge, new theater.

While the story line of the picture was compelling, it was the beauty of Montana that really struck me. I wondered to myself if the people of Montana would want the kind of attention the movie might attract. I mentioned it to Cameron, and he responded,

"Looks to me like there's plenty of room up there for everyone." There was simple logic to what he said, but he was still too young to understand what I was getting at. I asked

The Big Adventure

him if Montana looked like a place we should visit on our trip and he said, "Sure, Dad. It looks real pretty up there." I told him that such a big shift in direction might mean we wouldn't get to Los Angeles. Would he be O.K. with that?

His answer was quick and surprised me,

"I think I'd prefer going to places with fewer people." He had my attention. I responded,

"You sure about this? After all, you've been set on going to L.A. for quite a while."

"I'm fine with going up to Montana, Dad. It looks real pretty up there."

"O.K," I said, still taken aback by his response. "It's a go, then!"

After he fell asleep that evening, I sat quietly by the window, nursing a cup of coffee. I felt both relief and happiness that we would now be going north, not west, on our trip. I had not looked forward to LA traffic on a loaded bike. I wasn't sure why, but I knew this change in direction was right.

We hit The Tattered Cover in the morning with plans of each buying one book for the trip. Loaded to the max with luggage and camping gear, there was little room for more. Cameron picked a book on electronics (a big interest of his), and I chose a paperback copy of Thoreau's Walden, a book I hadn't read since college; but was drawn to when I saw it on the shelf.

I thought about what it would be like to live the simple life that Thoreau chronicled in his book. Short on money, yet long on self-reliance, his twenty-six months living in the small cabin he built on Walden Pond taught him about both himself and life. He was a complicated man living a simple life. I could only wish for the same. But was a simple life really possible? The kids, a mortgage, work, marriage, and all the trappings made for a life far from simple. The choices I'd made in life had resulted in many good things ... but also dealt its share of frustrations and pain. Like so many, I'd become caught up in the fast life, often reveling in my ability to not just keep the pace, but to set it. God, I knew I needed this trip. I wondered how much a soul could take before it was burned out or broken beyond repair. I just hoped it wasn't too late for me. I paid for the books, and we rode to the local Honda dealer.

The bike needed its 600-mile service. A new motor "machines" itself as it runs; leaving microscopic metal particles in the oil and making the initial oil change at 600 miles the most important one to the life of the engine. Sort of a metaphor for life--we take care of things early on and then begin to take them for granted over time as we wear down slowly into disrepair. Too little maintenance and our health, our work, and even our marriages, can begin to suffer. This trip was going to provide some much-needed servicing for my soul.

Finally, we headed west on I-70. The climb into the Rockies made an immediate difference in temperature. Well into the high 80's when we left Denver, it was closer to 70 degrees by the time we made Vail. Cool, but dry, we arrived comfortable, looking forward to a couple of days of mountain biking and relaxation in a beautiful part of the state. After checking into the Tivoli Lodge, a place our family had stayed on past vacations, Cameron asked to walk around the village by himself. He came back to the room after a while with a newly purchased cap gun and caps.

"Was that a smart way to spend your money, Cameron?" I asked sternly, mostly upset that he would waste his allowance on a toy that would lose its value almost immediately. His sad look showed his own recognition that perhaps he was too old for such a toy. I had an idea that this might be the time for a right-of-passage into young adulthood.

While he watched TV, I went out alone and bought him a large Swiss army knife at one of the outdoor stores and gave it to him over dinner at a local restaurant. I told him that I felt he was old enough to be trusted with such a tool. I was moved by his response as he came around the table to give me a big hug,

"I love you, Dad. You're right about the toy gun. I'm too old for that." I went through each tool on the knife, told him to be careful with it, and let him know that I trusted him with it. I could feel his pride as he showed the knife to the waitress.

"Wow, you're a lucky guy!" she said with an envious smile. "I was nineteen before I had one of those." Cameron's beaming smile showed a proud boy on his way to becoming a young man.

After three relaxing but active days in Vail, and five days total for the trip, we continued on our journey. The ride from Wolcott to Steamboat Springs on Highway 131 was beautiful and the weather perfect. At Craig, Colorado we turned north onto Highway 13, less than an hour from Wyoming. The bike, while running smoothly and effortlessly on six cylinders, was thirsty, forcing us to stop every 120-130 miles for fuel.

As we left the Elk Head Mountains, the terrain flattened out, and we began to sense the vastness of this part of the country. We only passed three vehicles in the forty miles to the Wyoming border.

It was a welcome stop at Baggs, WY, where we took on gas and soft drinks. I'd been pushing both of us to drink lots of water after feeling the effects of dehydration at 12,000 feet in the Colorado Mountains. The Iowa humidity we were used to was nonexistent in Colorado, something that agreed with me.

"From Iowa, huh?" I glanced up to see a young lady walking toward me. I placed the nozzle into the tank before realizing that this small station, in the middle of nowhere, was full service.

"Yup, a small college town called Grinnell," I replied with a smile.

"Hey, home of a great college there. I'm from Dubuque," she responded with little emotion.

"Pretty country up that way -- probably the prettiest part of Iowa," I said, as I continued the small talk. "What brings you way out here?"

"My husband works the oil fields," she responded matter-of-factly, and with a hint of discord. I left it alone and gave Cameron the money to pay inside. I fired up the big motor as the girl went back to her outdoor perch at the front of the station. There were two men sitting with her who hadn't moved but now shared a laugh with her as I, probably too carefully, turned the big bike around. I had no interest in laying down a bike that, loaded, weighed well over 900 pounds.

"How far to I-80?" I asked the group through the open visor.

"Fifty miles of nothing," the girl responded, now showing more than a hint of her dislike of this lonely country. I wondered to myself what it was like to live in such an isolated place. I asked Cameron, who had returned with a big smile and a large candy bar for himself, what he would think of living in such a place?

"At least they have TV," he said as he pointed to the roof of the building where, perched precariously, was an early-model satellite dish the size of a pitchers mound. I thought to myself that this trip was good for both of us and wondered if he could survive the trip without television. We pulled out of the station and pointed the bike north. As we accelerated through the gears, I felt thankful for our small town of Grinnell, and for the interesting and meaningful job I had.

After riding the fifty miles north on a barren two-lane highway, we traveled eighty-one miles west on I-80 to Rock Springs, Wyoming. I wasn't happy about being back on the big four-lane highway, but I knew we would soon exit the interstate and find a two-lane highway north.

The interstate highway system, bigger and faster than two-lane roads, was a perfect metaphor for America's growth. When we built those super highways, our goal was to get more people somewhere faster. That goal was accomplished, but to what end? Did we think about what we might miss along the way? For me, this trip was about slowing down, not speeding up, and about engaging with what was around us while on the trip.

Rock Springs made a good stopover spot as it was getting dark and we were both tired and thirsty. We camped at the Flaming Gorge National Recreation Area and watched the sun set before Cameron turned in early. I sat outside the tent at a picnic table thinking about the trip thus far and making the day's entry in my journal. We'd made a big shift in the direction of our trip. After weeks of planning for California and the west coast, we were now riding north. I still wasn't sure why the change, but did feel that we were being drawn north for a reason.

In the morning, after having breakfast at a roadside café, we began our ride up to Jackson to see both the Grand Tetons and Yellowstone Park over the next several days. The path from Rock Springs north to Jackson is through the Sweetwater Divide Basin. It was comfortable riding through open rolling countryside. The growing peaks of the Wind River Range were pulling us toward them like a magnet.

I could see darkening clouds ahead, and Pinedale offered us a chance to gas up and put on our rain gear for the first time. The first drops hit us as we rode toward the pass that would drop us down into Jackson. As we climbed, the drizzle changed to sleet. I knew we had to eventually drop down the slope and began hoping that the road surfaces would remain warm enough to keep us from losing traction. I was nervous. We were in the middle of nowhere, with no traffic around, and were on the verge of riding over a mountain pass through snow on a heavily loaded motorcycle. Not good.

"Are we gonna be O.K., Dad?" asked Cameron, clearly concerned.

"No problem, Bud. We'll be dropping down soon after going over the pass." I said it with far more confidence than I felt.

After we reached the pass, I slowed the bike to twenty miles per hour and we began to drop in altitude. As the elevation fell, the sleet turned back to rain, but picked up intensity. At least it was rain and not snow. Thankfully, the waterproof gear did its job.

Cold and tired from the tension of the ride, we finally rolled into Jackson, Wyoming. Famous for its cowboys and skiing, it was an interesting mixture of the past and present. After finding a room at a small motor court motel on the main drag, we unpacked, took hot showers and walked across the street to do laundry. After loading the washing machines, we walked around the town square to size up the place and do some people watching.

It was an interesting assortment of folks, broken into two clearly delineated groups: locals and outsiders. While many of the visitors were dressed in the appropriate local Western attire, one could easily tell that they weren't from the area. The locals had a way of both looking and feeling comfortable in their boots, jeans, and cowboy hats. The pretenders somehow couldn't find that comfort. Cameron and I fit somewhere in between as our outfits were a mixture of outdoor fleece and jeans with motorcycle boots. It could be that we stood out more than anyone.

We spent some time walking around the town learning of its history. While on one of these walks, I struck up a conversation with a local cowboy at an outdoor coffee bar as we both added cream to our coffees. I told him that it was pretty easy to see the difference between locals and visitors. He laughed, and said, "Look around you, the visitors are the ones with the double, non-fat lattes. The locals are drinking a simple cup of coffee." I smiled and nodded at the cowboy logic, glad that I had a regular cup of coffee in front of me. My new friend told me that he felt Jackson was losing its soul, catering to "big money and the ski crowd." I felt for him and could see the truth in what he was saying. The shops and restaurants were clearly attracting moneyed outsiders. I asked him if change could also be a good thing for the town, to which he replied,

"Not if it's shaped from the outside by folks who know nothing about the soul of the place." I was troubled by his reflection, as I could see how the very same thing has happened in many parts of our country, where history and traditions had been forgotten or overrun with the new. It reinforced to me that we live in a throwaway society where much of our past is lost in the race for progress. We continued to talk about lost values in America, and how we are advancing technologically at a far greater pace than we are spiritually. By the time he finished his coffee and left to return to work on his ranch, I felt concerned both for him and for my children. I knew that the next generation would suffer from this incongruence more than mine. As he walked off, I felt a pang of guilt as I realized I hadn't even asked his name.

After being holed-up in Jackson for a couple of days due to rain and cold weather, we finally made it through the Grand Tetons and Yellowstone Park. It was a chilly, yet beautiful ride. The cool weather kept the number of visitors down, and we had no problem with traffic as we stopped at many of the major spots in Yellowstone. We saw few people except at the park's major geyser, "Old Faithful." I wondered how many of these people had only stopped at Yellowstone's most famous spot on their drive through the park, seeing the rest of the park from the enclosed confines of their cars. "Another example of focusing on the end of the road, and not the path," I thought to myself. God knows we've all been guilty of that.

After two cycles of Old Faithful, Cameron was ready to move on. After a long day in America's first national park, we rode toward the east entrance and the long drop down to Cody, Wyoming.

The ride from the park brought a new and more beautiful mountain vista with every turn, prompting us to pull over often for pictures. The amazing scenery, smooth pavement, wide road and little traffic made for a dream ride. I felt at one with the bike as we made turn after turn in the long drop to the east entrance.

After a long day on the bike, we finally rode into the cowboy town of Cody, Wyoming and checked into a small hotel off the main drag. Cameron showered while I went across the street to gas up and wash the bike. After my own shower, we rode downtown to find a place to eat. We parked the bike on the street and entered the Irma Hotel to search out the burger Cameron was after.

As we entered the hotel and restaurant that Buffalo Bill Cody had built and named for his sister in 1902, I looked the place over, deciding against a table in favor of two open stools at the historic, beautifully-crafted wooden bar. I could tell this place was a local hangout. I smiled and nudged Cameron, pointing to a sign on the wall that said it all: *Nothing fancy, just good food.* The wood walls, ceiling of tin and wide-plank pine flooring gave the place a warm and natural feel; I could also feel the history of the place.

We saddled up at the bar and placed our helmets on the floor as a young, smiling waitress came over and welcomed us with two glasses of ice water. We thanked her and ordered Cokes and burgers. I settled down to look the place over as Cameron opened up the comic book he had bought in the motel shop. As I looked around, a man on the stool two seats down from us looked over and smiled, then asked,

"How's the search going?"

Great Thunder

I was a bit surprised by the question, and responded as if I wasn't sure of his meaning,

"What search is that?"

He continued smiling in a way that made me think he knew more about us than he should. He continued,

"We're all on searches aren't we? It's just that those on a big motorcycle are either searching for something or running from something. You look more like the former."

I answered his smile with my own as I took a good look at the man. He looked to be Native American, dressed in jeans, boots and a clean, pressed, white western shirt, much like every other cowboy in town. He was perhaps forty-five years old, I guessed to myself, as I sized him up.

"I suppose you've found me out," I responded, continuing to smile. "We're on a father-son trip."

"Iowa's a long way by bike, but then again, that's one big bike. I saw your license plate as you pulled up," he continued, answering my question of how he knew we were from Iowa.

"Yeah, it is a long way. We just came down from Yellowstone. It was a chilly ride up there, but it got warm in a hurry as we came down."

After a few seconds, he again asked, this time with piercing, yet compassionate eyes,

"So, how is the search going? I've yet to see someone who comes through here on a bike without a reason... especially on the kind of trip you're taking. Where are you headed next?" he asked directly.

"We hope to see as much of Wyoming and Montana as we can before heading home," I replied. "We're going to stay overnight here. We pushed it hard today to see as much of Yellowstone as we could."

"You picked a good place to rest," he said, as he smiled again. "Not a whole lot going on around here except the rodeo. They have one every night here. Folks come from all over for it."

"So we've heard. I expect we'll check it out," I replied, wondering who this man was. He seemed very relaxed and sure of himself.

I reached across the empty stool and offered my hand. He returned my handshake with a firm grip.

"I'm Will Freeman, from Grinnell, Iowa. I teach and coach at a small liberal arts college there."

His response surprised me,

"My people call me Great Thunder... but folks around here call me..." I interrupted him,

"Great Thunder is good enough for me if it is good enough for your people. This is my son, Cameron." I leaned back for him to get a look at my boy, still locked in his comic book.

He smiled and said, "Handsome kid." I could tell he was pleased that I accepted his Native American name. "So you teach?" he asked. "Then it seems we're in the same business." He paused for a moment before continuing, "I don't teach in a classroom, although I guess you could consider this place a classroom of sorts."

I nodded and said, "We were on the way to California, but got sidetracked down in Colorado. I guess your state was calling us and we chose to listen."

"The Rockies can do that to people," he replied with a smile, adding, "Sometimes things happen for a reason and we dismiss it as chance or dumb luck; but in fact, they happen because we finally listen to more than just our brain."

I nodded, saying, "It's funny, we did all this planning for weeks to get to California and then on up to Oregon. Then we felt this pull to turn the bike north. I'm still a bit surprised that we listened and changed our plans."

"How would you explain that pull?" he asked as the waitress brought us two of the biggest burgers I'd ever seen. He answered his own question with a knowing smile, "Perhaps a power greater than us wanted you to know that the purpose of your trip would be better found in Wyoming, and not California."

"I expect so," I answered as I lifted the giant burger, wondering how I could possibly get it into my mouth and not embarrass myself in the process. Cameron began his feast with delight.

"Dad, look at the size of this thing! This might be dinner and breakfast." Both Great Thunder and I smiled as we shared a look of appreciation for the innocence and honesty of youth.

I turned to Great Thunder and asked him if he was from the area.

"I grew up on a reservation in South Dakota. I left home when I was eighteen. There was nothing to keep me there. My parents had died, I had no brothers or sisters, and I saw no future on the reservation that didn't include drugs or alcohol, so I left. I got involved in rodeo and was able to make a pretty good living at it until I retired about twenty years ago."

"Twenty years ago?" I responded. "Kind of young to retire, wasn't it?"

"Not at all," he responded, as he smiled. "I was forty-five when I retired from the circuit." I let that sink in while I did the math a couple of times.

"That would make you about… sixty-five?" I asked with more than a little disbelief.

"Sixty-six next month," he responded with a smile.

"Man, you obviously know how to take care of yourself!" I said, amazed that this man could be sixty-five years old. He could have easily passed for forty-five.

I continued to eat the burger, hardly making a dent. I looked over at Cameron who had shifted his energy from the burger to the comic book, oblivious to my conversation with Great Thunder.

"So what have you been doing since your retirement from the circuit?" I inquired, wondering if I should ask such a personal question to someone I had just met.

"Oh, I sit around in various cafés offering advice to those who are looking for it," he replied with a knowing smile. "Actually, I don't have to work anymore, so I give my time to those who need my help. I spend a great deal of time on the reservation. There's much to do there, with many battles to fight against alcohol and drugs. I'm trying to help the young people regain some self-respect, and perhaps some hope for their future. Your people would call me a medicine man or a shaman. I prefer to just be called a man whose mission is to help others in need."

"Sounds wonderful," I responded. "I have a gut feeling you're making a difference. It must be hard for the young people on the reservation to find a place of balance between the old ways and the new. How do you deal with that?"

"It's not easy," he replied. "In fact, a lot of our people felt that I'd abandoned them and our ways to become part of the white man's world. Of course, I never abandoned anyone. I knew I would return and teach after I had learned everything I could off the reservation. I'm comfortable in doing what I've done. I feel that every decision I've made has helped me know myself better, thus helping me to help others."

"Your early retirement ... was it an injury?" I asked.

"No," he replied. "I just felt that the young people needed me more than I needed the rodeo life." I could tell he was being totally honest.

"Well, I need to move on," he said, as he got off his stool and threw a few bills on the counter. "This should cover your burgers. Welcome to Cody. I expect I'll be back here for lunch tomorrow if you gentlemen care to join me. I usually get here by 11:30."

"Thank you! We'd like that very much," I replied as I got up to again shake his hand. "It's been a real pleasure. Until tomorrow, then?"

"You fellas really should get over to the rodeo tonight. It's a great show," he said as he went out the door. I started to answer that we would, but he was already gone. I returned to the burger, lost in thought about the man I had just met, still amazed that he could be sixty-five years old.

We spent the rest of the afternoon looking over the historic town of Cody, WY, founded in 1896 by Buffalo Bill Cody. The history of its founder was evident everywhere. The Buffalo Bill Historical Center included four museums, and Cameron wanted to see them all. Our schedule for the next morning would be full.

That evening, we made our way to the western edge of town for the nightly rodeo. There were dozens of horse trailers in the big parking lot. The variety of license plates showed that cowboys and cowgirls had come from all over the West, and even Canada, for the event. We made our way to the ticket booth and into the stands. I wondered if we were the only two in the grandstand without cowboy boots and hats. Cameron noticed too, asking,

"Dad, can I get a cowboy hat?" I had to say "no" since we had little room to carry extra baggage, especially hats that would be crushed in the already-full luggage bags.

We enjoyed a great rodeo as the talented announcer led the crowd through the various disciplines of the sport, making it both exciting and funny at the same time. As we watched the performers, my mind returned to Great Thunder. Here was a man who gave up what was apparently a lucrative career in the rodeo to give back to his people. What strength it must have taken, I thought, to put others before himself. My encounter with this man prompted thoughts of the work of Abraham Maslow, the twentieth-century American psychologist, who theorized that self-actualization and meaning in life are intertwined. I had studied Maslow with great interest many years ago, agreeing that we do, in fact, grow through stages of personal development. After meeting the basic physical needs of living, we can then progress to meeting our psychological needs. The ultimate level of self-actualization is where we no longer are driven by our own selfish needs, instead living to give to others. In Great Thunder, I had met a man who was finding meaning in his life by helping other people. I wondered if I could ever attain such a level of growth. I had the impression that Great Thunder, himself, was developing on a personal level as he was helping others to grow and learn. My gut feeling was that this man had found real meaning to his life and I felt compelled to learn more about him. Our plan to leave town the next day was now off. We had a lunch date to keep.

After returning to the motel, Cameron parked himself in front of the TV. It had been a long and eventful day, and I knew he wouldn't last long. I was right. He was asleep within a couple of minutes. I covered him up with a blanket and moved outside onto the deck with a cup of coffee. I thought about the meeting with Great Thunder, wondering if it was chance, or something more, that had brought us together. Here was a man who had experienced much in his life, and, after having moved away from home to learn, had returned to help others. I got the distinct impression that he had learned what was important in life.

I turned off the light and lay down on the bed, thinking about the many turns my life had seen since I left my Kentucky home to see the world. I remembered the day when, as a young eighteen year-old, I boarded an airplane for the first time bound for college. I didn't just leave my hometown. I left all my friends and all the experiences that had shaped me to that point. The power of home is never as strong as when you have to leave it. My life was clearly about to change dramatically and I was scared to death, yet excited beyond words at the prospects for the future.

Even at that young age, I knew that life would never be the same as new doors opened up for me, both intellectually and athletically. I had spent my first eighteen years in Lexington, home of fast horses, great college basketball, and within sixty miles of where generations of my family had been born and raised. Reasonably gifted academically and more gifted athletically, I left Kentucky for Gainesville, Florida to make my mark as an athlete for the Florida Gators. From 1972 through 1980 I lived the life of a successful athlete, chasing fame and respect through the sport of pole vaulting. I was rewarded with worldwide travel, awards, and a free education. Still, I grew little in the ways that mattered most. I was determined to be the best at something, and I would do anything to make it happen.

The truth is I was driven to excel for all the wrong reasons, all of them external. While my athletic abilities soared, and the resulting recognition came, it never seemed to be enough. It wasn't often that I was truly happy. Success as an athlete gave me a "quick fix" of self-esteem as I rode a dangerous roller coaster of needing to have others affirm my worthiness and feeling the lowest of lows when I didn't get that affirmation.

After retiring as an athlete, I used the same drive and determination as a coach, but again with the same external motivations to affirm my worth as a person. Countless conference titles helped to do this, but again, with little lasting effect. I was now successful as a coach, but still fighting the need to prove myself to others. How difficult it is for us to accept ourselves, I thought, as I sipped the coffee. I've got to figure this out.

Exhausted from the taxing look into my past, I finally slept hard and without dreams.

The Teacher Becomes The Student

The next morning, I awoke early and left a note for Cameron saying that I would be back shortly. I took an early walk through the town deep in thought about the life I had chosen. I had left Kentucky a scared young man. I knew that I had to leave home to achieve my dreams as an athlete. I spent six wonderful years in Gainesville, Florida and traveled around the globe in pursuit of a dream I would never fully realize, that of becoming the best pole-vaulter in the world. I had lived the passion for my own athletic excellence, but it came at the expense of growth in other areas.

I returned to the motel, feeling an odd sense of fatigue at having spent so much time thinking at such a deep level. I would recognize later that it would in many ways mark a beginning for me. I wasn't sure of the meaning of meeting

The Big Adventure

Great Thunder, but I had a feeling that the reason would soon be revealed.

As I entered the room, Cameron was deep into cartoons. "Morning, Dad," he said.

"Hey Bud. Sleep well?"

I smiled as he said, "Yup," unable to look away from the screen. I walked to the bathroom and turned on the hot shower. My thoughts returned to yesterday's events as I stepped under the hot water. I began to make plans for the day: a trip to the Buffalo Bill museums and then lunch with Great Thunder.

We spent a great morning at the four museums learning about the histories of the West, firearms and of Native Americans. It was good to spend quality time with my oldest child. In no hurry, I let him take the lead. Cameron ate at the museum and requested that he go back to the room to watch some TV and read comic books. I wrote the phone number of The Irma Restaurant on a card, left it by the phone and turned to leave for my lunch with Great Thunder. Cameron was already lost in another cartoon. I said goodbye and closed the door. I heard him yell, "Bye Dad!" through the door as I walked away. As I mounted the bike, Cameron came out the door and walked over to me. He gave me a hug.

"Thanks for taking me to the museums, Dad. It was a lot of fun."

I was a bit surprised at the spontaneity of the moment and replied with a smile,

"My pleasure, Cam. The number to the cafe is by the phone if you need me. Make sure you lock the door and don't open it for anyone." I rode off thinking what a great moment that was, and wondered how many more of those I would experience before he would be too old to hug his dad.

When I entered the Irma, Great Thunder was sitting where he had been the day before.

"How's our biker from Iowa?" he asked with a smile.

"Just fine," I replied as I placed my helmet on the hat rack. "We had a good sleep after such a long day yesterday. We got to the rodeo last night, and then to the museums this morning. This town has a lot to offer for such a small place. Cameron was especially interested in the firearms and knife collections."

"Sometimes the best things come in small packages," he responded. He motioned to me to sit on the next stool and continued, "When I was a child, I remember seeing a knife in the hardware store window. It was the most beautiful thing I'd ever seen: a perfectly balanced German blade, beautifully carved bone handle and a hand-tooled leather holster for the belt. He lifted up his shirt and took the knife from its sheath and put it on the counter.

"This is it?" I asked as I looked at it.

"Yes," he replied. "Go ahead and pick it up." I carefully lifted it and looked at the most beautiful knife I had ever seen.

Great Thunder then continued with his story, "I would make up reasons to go in the store so I could see the knife, dreaming of what it would be like to own it, but knowing that would never happen. Our family had little money, and the knife was very expensive. Then one day, the knife was no longer in the case. It had been sold.

The Big Adventure

I was very sad. A few weeks later, I was shocked to open my birthday present and see the knife. My father told me that I had earned the knife. I wasn't sure how I'd earned it, but I was sure happy to have it. It was the most beautiful thing I had received in my young life. To this day, it's my most prized possession."

"Because it was from your father?" I asked.

"Yes," he replied, "but there's more to it than that. My father died many years ago, and before he passed, he told me why, and how, he had received the knife. He had heard from the storeowner that I'd had my eye on the knife for some time. I'd never asked to have it out of the case because I knew I could never afford it. Just prior to my twelfth birthday, the storeowner suffered a heart attack and was unable to tend his farm, which brought in most of his income. I had suggested to my father that we might harvest his crop for him, thinking that it might speed his healing. Father had asked me, 'Why do you want to help this man bring in his crop before harvesting our own.'
I told him, 'Because he's in greater need than us, Father.' My dad's smile told me I'd given the right answer. After the harvest, the storeowner had given the knife to my father with instructions to give it to me as a thank-you gift. My father gave it to me on my birthday, telling me that he had never been prouder of me because I had learned the most important of all lessons: putting others before ourselves is the greatest gift we can give. I carry the knife every day, because it reminds me of that lesson."

I took a moment to absorb the wonderful story and its meaning.

"Sounds like your father was a very good man," I said, respectfully.

"Yes, he was. No education in the classroom, but one of the wisest men I have ever known."

"I understand," I responded. "I expect there's a big difference between knowledge and wisdom. I'm well aware of how to gain knowledge. That's the business I'm in. I've learned, however, that wisdom doesn't come quite so easily."

Great Thunder responded quietly, but with conviction, "Wisdom does not come only from experience. It also comes from listening to your heart and soul, and not just your brain."

"Hard to disagree with that," I responded. "To become a shaman...I expect you must be trained. How does one end up in such a profession?"

Great Thunder smiled. "I'm not so sure it's a profession. It's more of a calling. When I was young, I was told by some of my elders that I had the skills to follow in the traditions of the medicine man. I wasn't sure what they meant, but I knew that it took great skills... skills I felt I didn't have. Still, I was honored that I would be chosen to carry on the traditions. A medicine man is chosen because of his character and actions. There must be evidence that he wants to help others. These skills cannot be used to better oneself, only to help others. When used for self-betterment, the skills simply will not work."

"So you were chosen to do this?" I asked.

"More like it chose me," he responded with a smile. "Like I said, my elders knew when I was young that I was someone who might continue the traditions."

"I'm guessing you could write quite a book about the experiences you've had."

"I suppose I could. There have been many. In most people's eyes these experiences would be viewed as good, bad, perhaps even amazing... but to me, they were just what they were. Our people see a value in all experiences. There is a lesson in everything that happens, every circumstance, in every moment, in every meeting of a person."

I nodded, now believing that my meeting this man was likely to offer me a special opportunity to learn. I was beginning to see that this was a unique person indeed. We ordered lunch as the topic changed from Great Thunder to our bike trip. I explained that we were on a father-son adventure, while all of the girls were on their vacation to Holland.

"My boy is growing up so fast," I said. "He amazes me with his many talents, yet I think the next few years will be tough for him as he tries to find his identity. There is so much outside stuff going on that can shape how he thinks and who he is."

Great Thunder listened, took a drink of water and responded,

"He has an identity. He's had that from the beginning. When we are born we have a very pure identity, every one of us absolutely unique. Our lives are like a big classroom. There are good experiences and bad, and all of them offer lessons and tests. But at his age, young people think only in black and white terms. Things are only good or bad, and they only want to experience the good. This is an alien concept to my people. We see all experiences, good and bad, as part of the process of learning. We learn from it all. Those who have not faced adversity have not experienced what it takes to become a warrior."

Great Thunder continued as I listened intently, "I've had two great teachers, both highly respected medicine men. Both were elderly and had experienced much. The process I went through to become fully trained in the ways of our medicine occurred when I had returned to my people after I was done with rodeo."

"How long did the training take?" I asked.

"It still goes on," he replied with a smile. "I continue to learn from everyone I meet. I expect you, too, will have something to offer me."

"I doubt that," I responded with a smile.

He was quiet for a moment and looked directly into my eyes.

"Let me ask you a question. What is your greatest challenge as a teacher and coach of young people?"

I smiled, responding,

"You kind of get right to the point, don't you?"

"We have to," he responded, smiling again. "You folks may not be here long, and the clock is ticking."

"And how will I pay you for your advice?" I asked.

"By returning the favor to others, when an opportunity arises," was his immediate response.

So, after a moment to think, I began,

"OK, well, I expect my biggest challenge is helping people realize their potential, and, hopefully, to prepare them for what comes after sport. We take someone with potential and try to help them develop, to experience ... and hopefully, to learn something about themselves in the process."

Great Thunder nodded and asked,

"And do you accomplish this admirable goal?"

"Not always," I replied, smiling. "Some athletes are more coachable than others, and some did a better job of picking parents ... meaning they have a better genetic predisposition for success. Add to that the athlete's psychological makeup, personality traits, motivations, discipline, emotional baggage and the like. Actually, there are a lot of things that contribute to a successful experience. A lot of folks think that coaching is easy; we just click the stopwatch and tell them to run. Of course, it's a far more complicated process than that."

"And where does the coach fit into it all?" he asked with perfect bluntness.

"Well," I responded, "The coach needs to be knowledgeable, to be able to communicate, to lead, and to show a real concern for the athlete. And I think, at some point, we have to know when to get out of the way."

"So a bond of trust must be developed between you and the athlete for success to occur?"

"Absolutely," I responded.

"So the purpose is to help them not just perform at a higher level, but to grow to a higher level?" he asked, more as a statement than a question.

"Yes, I try for that," I replied.

We both ordered salads as the waitress poured our coffee. Great Thunder continued,

"Have you ever heard of Abraham Maslow?"

"Wow, this is strange," I answered. "I was just thinking about him last night; the first time I've thought about his work in a very long time. You've read him?" I asked.

"Yes," he answered. "I know his work well. Maslow theorized that if you don't get enough of something, you feel a need, and continue to feel that need until it is satisfied. At the lowest level, there are the physiological needs of breathing, drinking, eating, getting rest, avoiding pain, and satisfying sexual urges. If you think about it, the saliency of the need is in that order. In other words, the needs as I mentioned them, take precedence over the one that follows. You may be very thirsty for instance, but if you are having trouble breathing, the need for air takes priority over the need for water."

I nodded, as I wracked my brain to remember what I could about Maslow.

"I get the feeling you have done some studying in philosophy and psychology."

"Part of my search," he replied with a smile. "After the physiological needs are met, the individual progresses to other levels; safety needs, belonging needs, and esteem needs. Once we are in a safe environment, we can focus on being a social animal and on respecting others and ourselves. Of course, before we can gain self-confidence and ultimately freedom, we have to go through the process of achieving status and fame, of gaining attention and appreciation from others. In other words, we have to get others to respect us before we can gain self-respect."

"Seems kind of backwards, don't you think?" I interjected.

"Exactly. If people could first accept themselves, then they could give so much more to others."

I nodded in affirmation,

The Big Adventure

"This is great stuff. I wish we had the time to really talk about the issues I face in coaching others, and the issues I face..."

"On a personal level?" he said as he finished my statement.

I nodded.

"How long do you have?" he asked quietly.

"... I don't know. Actually, we could probably stay as long as we need to. The girls are in Europe for several more weeks and we have no set itinerary."

"Then we will meet until you have what you need from me."

I pondered his answer.

"Why are you doing this for me?" I asked. "How will I repay you?"

"Like I said before, you will repay me by teaching others. I have the feeling you will be sharing what you learn. This isn't about payment, only about growing and sharing." He smiled and said something that made chills run up my spine,

"You changed your trip to come this way for a reason. I've been chosen to be the one to show you the way. There are things you need to learn, and it won't be easy for you. You want to be better at this coaching. But first you will need to be better at being you. That is where we will focus."

After a moment to digest his words, I said,

"When do we start?"

He answered,

"Tomorrow. I'll meet you here at eight for breakfast."

"I have a feeling this won't be of much interest to Cameron," I said.

"I think we can take care of Cameron for a couple of days," he responded. "A close friend and his business partner have a ranch just a few miles from Cody. It's a working dude ranch. Families come in and stay for days at a time. Parents sometimes also send a child alone for a few days. It is a great learning experience. Think he might be interested?"

"I'll bounce it off him and let you know at breakfast," I responded, wondering if Cameron would want to do this alone. I finished eating as Great Thunder asked,

"Before you leave today, I want you to think about something."

"Alright," I responded, a bit wary of what was to come.

"Do you think of others before yourself?"

I just nodded, unsure of how to respond. He wrote a phone number on a card and gave it to me.

"Talk things over with Cameron and call this number later today. They can get things set up for tomorrow." He laid down some bills on the counter, slid off the stool and tipped his cap.

"Breakfast is on me. See you in the morning, Coach. Give some thought to my question."

I nodded in return and watched him leave the café, wondering what the next few days would hold for me.

When I returned to the room, I spoke with Cameron about the prospect of a couple of days at the dude ranch and of learning to ride a horse. He jumped up from his chair and hugged me,

"I was hoping I could do something cool like that, Dad!"

I then explained that I was going to be meeting with a "special teacher" while he was at the dude ranch.

"Are you OK with my staying in Cody, while you are at the ranch for a couple of days? You will have my phone number. I found out that there are other boys up there doing the same thing."

"I really want to do this, Dad," he said again, as he hugged me again.

I called the number and got things set up. Later that day, we walked to a nearby Western clothing store. No cowboy on a dude ranch could be without a cowboy hat and boots. We'd figure a way to lash them to the bike for the trip to Iowa.

Cody, Wyoming had begun as a stop for a hamburger. I could now see that we were pulled here for another reason, something far more important.

Part Two

Let the Learning Begin

Sometimes dreams are wiser than waking
Oglala Sioux saying

We had a wonderful prime rib dinner at the Irma Restaurant, loading up with large helpings. Cameron was giddy with excitement as we returned to the hotel. After watching a movie, we retired early, both looking forward to the next day. I lay wide-awake as Cameron slept, wondering what was in store for both of us. I still couldn't believe that we were doing all this. We were committed now, and while I was excited, I couldn't shake an underlying fear of what I might face. Finally, exhausted, I fell into a deep sleep.

In the morning, I called Great Thunder, and he joined us at a small café-bakery on the main drag of Cody. He told Cameron that he would be working hard as a junior cowhand at the ranch and gave him a pair of new deerskin gloves saying, "You'll need these to protect those hands."

After breakfast, we loaded up his gear and took him out to the ranch. As we checked in, Cameron met another boy his age, named Allen, who was also there for the same experience. The two hit it off and were told they would be bunking together in the bunkhouse. I was glad that he would have a new friend to share the experience with. Cameron gave me a tentative hug, saying, "I don't think cowboys give hugs, Dad."

I smiled as he turned to walk back to the bunkhouse for an orientation session with the other young people. I felt a lot more comfortable as I watched him walk off, almost wishing that I could join him; but then, I knew my own experience was calling. As he continued to walk away, I yelled to him that I would call him each day to see how it was going.

"Oh, that's OK, Dad. I don't think the other guys will have their parents doing that." I smiled, thinking he was wrong about that.

"You call me if you need me," I yelled after him. "I'll see you in a couple of days, four o'clock right here." I waved and turned and walked to the bike.

I mounted the bike and followed Great Thunder's pickup away from the ranch. We drove for about half an hour up into the foothills of the mountains via Highway 120 and then onto the Chief Joseph Highway. We began a long climb of switchbacks. We pulled off the road onto a gravel drive, continuing at a much slower pace for another fifteen minutes. Finally, as I wondered how high this road could go, we came to a small pristine log cabin that was surrounded with greenery and endless red Wyoming Paintbrush, the Wyoming state flower. I was amazed at this colorful little sanctuary in the midst of a dry, high desert. We were at the end of the gravel road.

Let the Learning Begin

"Wow, this is gorgeous!" I said as I got off the bike. "No wonder the road has ended here. I think this might be heaven's gate!"

"Pretty, isn't it? But that is even more gorgeous," Great Thunder said as he pointed behind me. I turned and looked at the most beautiful vista I had ever seen: endless mountain ranges, a river far below, and not a house to be seen. I was speechless as I let the moment sink in. Finally, I spoke.

"So, This is your place?"

"Yes," he answered. I've been here for several years. I built the cabin with my own hands on the land I bought from my rodeo earnings."

"How do you get greenery and flowers to survive up here?" I asked.

"Only certain plants and flowers will make it up here. A brook behind the cabin gives me plenty of clean water for drinking and watering the plants. I like having lots of plants around -- good for the soul," he said with a smile.

"It feels good here," I said, as I continued to marvel at the view.

"Yes, I felt the same way when I first saw the site. That's why I finally bought the land and built the cabin. I camped initially, and felt a real sense of spirituality when here. When I finally decided to build, I first prayed for several days asking if it was OK for me to move forward with the project. I didn't want to force myself onto the land without clearance from a higher order." He smiled as he said it.

My respect for my new friend was increasing. He said,

"Why don't you relax into the place and look around. I'll make us some hot tea. Feel free to come on in and take a look around. Make yourself at home."

As Great Thunder went into the cabin, I walked around and marveled at both the landscaping and the cabin. It was clear that he had poured himself into this place with both love and hard work. As I looked closely at the cabin exterior, I could see that the workmanship was first-rate. This man knew woodworking! Every joint, the window trim, the shake roofing, everything that my eye could see exhibited extraordinary workmanship. As I walked to the back of the cabin, I was in for an even bigger surprise … the cabin was both wind and solar powered. With a stream out back and this equipment, he needed little else to live self-sufficiently off the grid. My best guess was that the cabin was about 20' x 40' in size, perfect for a mountain hideaway. I continued my walk around the place, finding my way back to the amazing view out front. As beautiful as the cabin was, the view was almost beyond words. I stood for a few moments as I took it all in. The green valley far below contrasted with snow-topped mountain ranges as far as one could see. Finally, I turned and stepped up to the small front porch and knocked on the door.

"No need to knock. Come on in, Coach."

I opened the screen door and walked in. The workmanship inside was equally remarkable. I marveled at the warm feeling it gave me.

"You built all of this?" I asked, in wonderment.

"Yes, everything you see is handmade, the cabinets, floors, all of it. I just tried to build to the level of the beauty of the place. It took three years to get it to what you see." He gave me a cup of tea in a beautiful glazed cup.

"I'm guessing you made this, too?" I asked with a smile.

"No," he responded with a laugh. "A lady friend of mine from down in Cody made a full set for the cabin. She often comes up here to meditate. A fine lady and a good soul."

We went out to the porch and sat on handmade Adirondack-style chairs facing the vista beyond. My thoughts drifted to Cameron, wishing he could see this place. I wondered to myself what he was doing at this moment. Great Thunder read my mind and said,

"I wouldn't worry about Cameron. He's in good hands and will have a great time on the ranch. It'll be a wonderful growth experience for him."

I responded, "I hope so. He's at an age when he is forming values that will shape his life in the future. Young people his age can't live without TV, computers and computer games. It all seems a bit superficial, if not downright detrimental. Television and the internet are shaping our kids' values. I also worry about the friends he hangs out with. He's a year younger than most of them and I worry that they might influence him in the wrong way. I'm hoping this experience at the ranch will be good for him."

"It's a big challenge, raising children in this day," he responded. "One of the big conflicts we face is living the manmade life. It's often at odds with our spiritual development. Have you ever been to New York City?"

"Yes, several times," I responded.

He continued, "Remember what it felt like when you first saw the Empire State Building?"

"Yes, it was mighty impressive, kind of like seeing the Golden Gate Bridge for the first time, both amazing testaments to engineering and to man's potential."

"No doubt," Great Thunder responded. "Now look out there," he said as he pointed to the spectacular view. "How would you compare this to the Empire State building and the Golden Gate Bridge?"

I thought for a moment and said, "I guess they don't really compare. One is about something man-made, and the other God-made. I guess it is hard to compare the two."

He responded, "Well-put. The problem is that our lives most often dwell in the man-made realm. Folks try to balance the realities of a pressure-filled, time-driven life with a spiritual commitment. Many try to find a sense of spirituality by going to church on Sundays, but are often unable to live that spiritual life through the week. Thus, spirituality becomes a part-time thing for many people, not a way of life. The bottom line is that it's hard to find a sense of contentment in our lives without developing ourselves spiritually. Have you ever wondered why so many people like to vacation and camp in a natural environment?"

Answering his own question, he went on, "I live up here for a reason. It provides me with a sense of peace and a sense of spirituality that I cannot find in a city. Many folks in the city are in a race, the rat race. Living a life that is driven from outside influences and pressures is a powerful thing that we are not very good at resisting. The sad part is that we often don't realize that we're increasing the pace at which we live. We just get caught up in the business of our lives and don't stop to think about whether it is right or not. Once we get on board, it's a hard train to get off. We begin to lose sight of what matters; lost marriages, problematic relationships with children, and a myriad of health problems are often the result. None of it is good. The bottom line is that we're driven by our man-made lives. Some will realize it and give it up to keep their family, their health, and their sanity. I was never driven by the need for success and all the trappings. I got what I needed from my rodeo days and then I left that life behind. It wasn't difficult. I just knew that I needed to go. I haven't missed it. What I do now is more important than rodeo. It's really pretty simple for me."

I listened with great interest, seeing the truth in what Great Thunder said. I thought to myself about what drives our lives. We live in a society driven by outside motivations. Life is measured by what we accomplish, how much we make and who we know. Living in a free enterprise society, our accomplishments are often a function of competition with others. And of course, winning just drives us to want even more. It was easy to see how things could accelerate out of control.

"When I bought this land, I did it within the white-man's laws. I had to purchase it from a realtor. I paid for it up front, built the cabin up to all the codes and, of course, pay taxes on it every year because it is not on tribal land. The Native American and the white man differ when it comes to land ownership. The white man has historically believed that land is available to acquire by anyone with enough money. History has also shown that the white man could acquire land by force, if necessary. If you have enough money or power, you can get what you want. That was the story of the Old West. My people see it differently. We believe that the land belongs to no man, but to the Great Spirit. We see ourselves only as short-term tenders of the land. We see the Great Spirit, who you would call God, in all of nature: all of the land, trees, and even the rocks. I feel a special spirit in this place, and I know it is the spirit of God at work. Nature is our church. I'm glad to see that the white man is now starting to recognize the damage being done to Mother Earth and is making strides to repair the damage. This damage to the earth has been very hard for our people to accept."

I could tell that the subject was painful as he continued, "My ancestors would often move with the seasons. When they would pack up to move on, they would leave the land as they had found it. When they hunted, they first prayed and asked the Great Spirit for success. They also gave thanks to the animal being hunted. After the kill, they used virtually the entire animal; there was little wasted. This was very different from the white man, who was only concerned with getting what he wanted. For many years, the plains were littered with skinned buffalo carcasses. It was about making money, or the sport of it all. It was a sad time for my people. When I was a young boy, my great grandfather told me stories of what it was like being a Native American in the late 1800s. He spoke of those times with great reverence and pride. I could feel his pain as he told me of what he had witnessed. His stories have stuck with me. Through his humility and honesty, I saw the truth. It made me very proud to be his descendent."

"I can tell you're proud of your family and your heritage," I said.

"Yes," Great Thunder said quietly. He was deep in thought as he looked at me and said, "My goal is to share with you some of the virtues and values of Native American people. You're an educator who can make a difference with the young people you work with. You can share these things in the way you teach. As I mentioned before, you are here for a reason ... and this is it." After a few moments of silence, he asked,

"Are you willing to listen and learn?"

"Yes." I answered. "I'm still not sure why I've been chosen for this, but I'm willing to give it a try."

"Good," he responded. "Let's get started. I've already told you of the first and most important value, 'to think of others before ourselves.' I told you the story about how I obtained this special knife. It's one example of how our people take care of others. We're willing to help those in need with no expectation of anything in return. It's simply something we are taught as children. What I didn't know as a child, but later learned, is that helping others without expectation will always result in something good happening to us."

After a few quiet moments, he asked,

"Have you given some thought to my question of yesterday? Do you think of others before yourself?"

"Honestly?" I responded after a few seconds, "I don't do enough of that. If I'm anything, I'm selfish. It does make me feel good when I do think of someone else first, but I can't say I am very good at it ... or that I do enough of it."

"I appreciate your honesty, Coach. Don't beat yourself up over it. You are here to try to understand yourself. We are all selfish on many levels. It's part of the human condition.

Truth is, selfishness is almost a prerequisite for survival. It's rooted in the survival instinct, the old survival of the fittest concept. You've obviously heard the saying *'looking out for number one'*, right?"

I nodded as he continued,

"Power and money have always controlled societies, and those who have those two things do not give them up easily."

I thought about my own selfishness and how much pain it had likely caused for others in my past. After a few moments, Great Thunder poured some more tea into my cup and asked,

"How did you begin coaching?"

I smiled as I thought of my initial years as a young coach, and began to tell Great Thunder my story.

After my first four years at Grinnell, it was clear that I wasn't very good at coaching. I had worked my track team down to last place at the conference meet, the first time any coach had finished last in my school's 100-year history of the sport. I wasn't proud of it, and, of course, was quick to rationalize and project my failure onto the athletes. It's human nature to take credit for our successes and, likewise, to blame others for our failures. I felt that a lack of effort, commitment and discipline on the part of my athletes was the root cause of the team's failure. It certainly couldn't have been me. I'd been a successful athlete who knew what it took to succeed. I knew *The Way*, but the athletes wouldn't follow. I would soon find out that I didn't have a clue about *The Way*. I needed to learn a whole lot more about Grinnell, and about myself, before I could hope to make a difference to my athletes.

Let the Learning Begin

After those dismal first four years, when we went from the middle of the conference to last, I had finally had enough. I went in to see our athletic director, John Pfitsch, the man who had hired my wife and me to coach at Grinnell. I was nearly in tears as I told him that I had to leave and I had determined that coaching was not for me. I wanted to go back to school, a safer haven for my ego. We had initially come to Grinnell between my Master's and Doctoral work, interested in taking a year's break from schoolwork, and perhaps making a little money in the process. As poor graduate students, the prospect of having any money was enticing. I told him that I could not take any more of the coaching. Having been to the mountaintop as an athlete, I knew what it took for success to occur and I felt my athletes did not have that same drive. He listened intently and then quietly asked me what my wife would think. While I had been floundering as a coach, she had been ultra-successful. I responded selfishly and with little emotion, "I'm leaving, John. She'll go with me."

Quiet for a few moments, John finally said, "Let's go down to the north classroom. We should talk in a more private setting." We went into that room at nine in the morning, closed the door, and did not emerge until nearly two in the afternoon. It was the hardest five hours of my young life. My mentor spoke to me with brutal honesty.

"You're a hot dog," he began. "Because you were a top athlete, you thought you could be a top coach ... as if it were that simple."

He went on to tell me that I was after success, not for the athletes, but for me. When we did poorly, it was a reflection on me as a person. I was coaching for selfish reasons. In a nutshell, our program was about me, and not the athletes.

"You have a lot of talents, young man, but you're misguided," he had said. "You don't care enough about the athletes. Your program has been about you, and that's the problem. At this college, it is about them, not you. Your wife figured that out early, and that's why she's winning conference championships. She's helping them to win by helping them to grow. She's motivating them to want to be better. Your method of motivation isn't working. I know you want to win, but an approach where results takes precedence over a healthy process, will not work here, at least not consistently over time."

Over those several hours in that classroom, we talked about the things that matter in life, including how sport and competition promote a win-at-all-cost mentality.

"That attitude belongs at the Division I level where you were trained," John had said with a caring smile. "Son, this level of sport is about the development of the person first, the athlete second. When you show them you are doing this for them, they'll respond." I knew he spoke the truth. He had experienced the highest level of collegiate sports himself. Before coming to Grinnell College, he had been Dr. Forrest "Phog" Allen's first assistant basketball coach at Kansas University. Now, after thirty years as the athletic director at Grinnell College, I knew that he understood all levels of the collegiate sport experience. More importantly, he understood people.

I was nearly in tears as I realized how I must have come across to my athletes. He went on, "Our cross country coach

Let the Learning Begin

is giving up his position to focus on his other duties at the college; I was hoping you might leave football and take the cross country position. It might provide some continuity for your track program." He paused, and then added, "It also might be a way to start over."

I mulled his offer over for a few days. I felt burnt out and didn't want to jump into something else that might be more painful to me. I also knew, however, that my wife was happy at Grinnell and wanted to stay. I was scared silly as I later told John that I would accept his offer to take the cross country program, and that we would stay, at least for a while. I knew nothing about distance running, but I would give it a try. That difficult decision would change my life, as it forced me to not only learn a new sport, but to learn how to be a better coach. John had been right. My approach to coaching had been wrong ... very wrong, and selfishness and poor self-esteem were at the root of it.

Great Thunder listened to my story only stirring to get up for more tea.

"Why did you feel the need to prove yourself as a coach?" he asked.

"Because those who succeed are respected in our society. People like winners. All of us need to have others like us and respect us. Maybe it was just an inherent need to prove myself to others."

"So, you must win to be respected?" he quickly asked.

"Winning does make it easier. We live in a society that values success. Whether that success is winning athletic contests or making a lot of money, we like winners."

For a few moments, Great Thunder looked right through me, then said,

"This is a major difference between the white man's values and my people's values. We view honor above the accumulation of material things. Our ultimate success is in living a life of honor. We are not against wealth, if it is attained with honor, and if we can then help others who are less fortunate. You were going through a time where you were looking for others to validate you. Of course, ultimately, you found that only **you** could do that. You showed great courage in staying at your school. I believe this man, your athletic director, was a true friend and mentor to you. Only a real friend will tell us the truth ... even when it hurts."

"Yes," I said. "John had been down the path for many years, and understood the things that mattered. I learned, over time, that being a good coach was very different than being a good athlete. All the same, it did hurt to hear him tell me the truth."

Great Thunder thought quietly for a moment and then said,

"We get better at what we do when we get better at being who we are." He continued, after giving that thought a moment to sink in, "So things improved for you after your talk?"

"Yes," I responded. "It was almost shocking how fast it changed." I went on to explain how I had set up a May meeting with the young men who would be on my first cross country team that upcoming fall. I chose to sit with them in a circle, rather than address them from a podium. I told them that I knew little or nothing about the sport and I

Let the Learning Begin 57

would need their help to make it work. It would have to be a true team effort. I said that each of them would have to be an active player in the process. I also said I would study and learn to be the best coach I could. I asked them to forgive me for being a self-centered jerk and told them I wanted them to be successful ... for them! I think they were a bit surprised, having gone through four years of my dysfunctional coaching. To make a long story short, they placed fourth in conference that fall (my first season as the coach), took second in conference the following year, and then began a long string of conference wins."

"What single thing made the biggest difference?" Great Thunder asked.

"That's easy," I said, "I simply began looking at things from the athlete's perspective, instead of mine. The process became athlete-centered instead of coach-centered."

"Meaning what?" he asked, as he lifted his cup of tea.

"Well, in a coach-centered model, everything is done from the coach's point of view. Communication is a one-way process; often limited to the coach's knowledge base. Goals are often dictated by the coach, with little or no athlete input. Of course, our natural tendencies are to work toward autonomy and independence. Since a coach-centered model won't allow for that kind of growth, it creates tension between coach and athlete, often becoming adversarial."

"And how does this coach-centered model compare to your athlete-centered model?" he asked, taking another sip of tea, but keeping his eyes trained on mine.

I responded, "In the athlete-centered model, communication becomes a two-way process, with performance goals based on the athlete's input and his or her own values and desires. Goals are correlated to the athlete's life mission. The development of the individual becomes the primary emphasis, not the athletic accomplishment. I guess the biggest difference is that the coaching process becomes two-way, with both parties offering input in a relationship that leads the athlete to independence, not dependence. It's just a healthier model of coaching. My experience with both has validated that for me."

"Very impressive, Coach. It seems your model is one based on respect and personal validation. It sounds like a healthy process. Do you think it would work at all levels of sport?"

"I think it has potential to, but it would require the right relationship between coach and athlete. Both have to be ready for it. The athletes have to be prepared to take ownership, to take the lead, so to speak. The coach, likewise, has to be ready to progressively give up ownership of the process as the athlete grows in independence and leadership. I think it takes a lot of courage for a coach to give ownership to the athletes. Coaches' jobs are on the line, and they have to succeed to keep those jobs. Most don't have the luxury of a lot of time to find success. Frankly, it's kind of risky to give up control to the athlete."

"Don't you have to succeed at your level of sport to keep your job?" he asked.

"Yes, but I think we have to be careful in how we define success. We try to offer a product to the athletes, one that helps them grow. Ultimately, growth is more important than winning. Don't get me wrong. I like to win. I prefer to win.

Let the Learning Begin

But I can sleep at night when we don't, because I think I see the bigger picture. My job is to help the athletes get the most out of their talents, provide a positive learning experience, and to do it with honesty and integrity. I believe that if we do those things, we will experience our share of success."

"I'm impressed, Coach," said the wise one. "How do your professional colleagues view this kind of teaching model?"

"I'm not real sure, actually. I do speak at many coaching clinics about these concepts, but I always tell the audience that the purpose of the material is to make them think. I don't try to sell anyone. I think all coaches and teachers have to find their own path. I just want the other coaches to let the concepts percolate for a while. Then they can make a judgment if it will work in their situation. Like I said, some are ready, some are not. I was ready because my coaching had hit bottom. I had no other direction to go but up, so it was easy for me to try something new. All I know is that there is truth in this teaching model, at least for me. Others have to find their own truths."

Great Thunder nodded in affirmation as he walked to the kitchen,

"How about some great apple pie?" he asked. "The lady who made the cups also makes the best apple pie you've ever tasted."

"Sounds great," I responded.

As Great Thunder cut the pie into large slices, he continued,

"You spoke of integrity. When I was seven years old, my grandfather took me to my first rodeo, down in Arthur, Nebraska. I was hooked from the moment we entered the arena. The colors, the pageantry, the announcer; it was quite an experience for a young boy who had never been off the reservation. It was a small town, but a big rodeo. After a full evening, we stopped at a café to have a late dinner. After eating, grandfather gave me some money and told me to go to the counter and pay the lady for the meal. I did so, bursting with pride that I'd be given the responsibility for such an important job. I paid the lady and put the change and the receipt in my pocket, returning to the table. My grandfather, in the middle of telling a story, did not ask for the money.

Later, perhaps fifteen minutes down the road, he remembered and asked for the money and receipt. I gave it to him and he counted it out. I noticed that he shook his head and quietly re-counted the money. He then asked our friend to turn the car around and return to the café. He had not been given the correct change. So we turned around and retraced our path to the café. When we arrived, I was nearly in tears as I asked him forgiveness for not getting the proper change. I knew how hard he worked for what little money he had.

He looked at me and quietly said,

'Don't be troubled, Great Thunder. It's not your fault. Come inside with me as I straighten this out.' When we got inside, my Grandfather met with the lady who took our money at the register.

'Hello, young lady. I'm sorry for troubling you, but you seem to have given my grandson too much money back when he paid you a few minutes ago.'

'I did?' she responded.

Grandfather continued, 'It would be wrong to have your books come up short at the end of the evening. I expect you would be responsible for the missing money.'

'Thank you so much, sir. It is good to know there are still honest people out there,' she said. 'How much was I off on the bill?'

'You gave us back one dollar too much by mistake.' He gave her the dollar. She thanked him again and gave me a wink as we left.

As we walked to the car, I asked Grandfather why we had come all the way back for just one dollar.

Grandfather said something that has always stuck with me. 'Integrity has no dollar amount. The right thing was to bring the money back, regardless of the amount. We become better people for doing what is right.'

To this day, I think about that experience often. We probably spent more than a dollar on gas getting back to the café. Still, he was adamant about doing the right thing ... and, perhaps, about showing me what integrity was all about. It has stuck with me all these years. Having integrity means we have to answer, not just to a higher authority for the decisions we make, but to ourselves."

"That's a wonderful story," I said, as I marveled at how his grandfather had used the situation to teach a life lesson about integrity.

Great Thunder continued,

"My grandfather had a special way of using life's events to help shape my character and values. Do you ever think of integrity in the coaching process?" he asked.

I thought for a moment, and said,

"Unfortunately, it's usually the lack of integrity that makes more headlines than integrity. I expect cheating is a part of the human condition. I try to see integrity in a more elemental way than that. Integrity has to do with the actual process. Are the training elements, no matter how small, done with integrity and done well? Is the training done in a way that reflects a sense of quality and honor toward the sport, the team and the coach? I've found that success comes from taking care of the little things, the day-to-day, mundane elements of training. When the little things are done with integrity and passion, and done well, they build a foundation for self-confidence in the athlete. This self-belief must be there if success is to occur consistently. Sometimes this can take some time because the athletes are often still developing physically when we get them. But, if they have patience, and show integrity to the training process, they can, in time, be successful. More importantly, I think they develop a strong work ethic, discipline and persistence, all values that are important to a successful life. That's where the long-term benefits occur."

"I like that," Great Thunder said with a smile. "I can see that a healthy process is important to your coaching."

I nodded and continued,

"Honesty and integrity are hard to come by these days. Everyone wants a piece of the proverbial pie with little regard for doing what is right. I'm afraid we're losing our integrity as our technological development outpaces our spiritual development." I told Great Thunder about my conversation with the cowboy in Jackson, the topic being the same disconnect between technological development and spiritual development.

"Unfortunately, you're right," he said. "Spiritual development has taken a backseat to our technologically-driven lifestyle. The pace of today's life is often without honor or integrity. We reinforce and rationalize these kinds of behaviors as being acceptable, then pass them on to our young. People then repeat the same. A lot of my medicine deals with these issues. A lack of spiritual development often leads people to escape when they have trouble dealing with the pressures of life. Alcohol and drugs have become major enemies of my people, if not all people."

I nodded, listening intently as he continued,

"In the Indian culture, many of our young people will face questions about their own place in this world by experiencing a Vision Quest. Are you familiar with the Vision Quest?" he asked.

"Sort of," I answered, knowing that I was not being fully honest. He sensed my lack of knowledge on the topic and went on,

"A person will go out into nature, far from the man-made life, to commune with the earth and the Great Spirit and to face core questions about the purpose of his life. Totally alone, he will undertake the Quest without food, with only water and the bare necessities for survival. It's a powerful experience, and one that changes young people into adults." He looked right at me, and what he said next hit me with a jolt.

"Coach, you will be called to do a Vision Quest. Not now, but in the future. I will say nothing more of this, but you should honor that calling when it comes."

I simply nodded, not sure how to respond. I did notice that the hair on my arms was standing up. I acknowledged it to Great Thunder,

"Why do I feel a sense of fear as you say these things?"

"There's good reason to fear, Coach. You're on a search for integrity, a search for meaning. Your motorcycle trip is just the beginning. There will be many fearful moments ahead, but by facing these moments you will develop courage. It is these moments that will give you the answers you seek. Again, you will know when the time is right. The Quest will call you to it."

"Did you experience a Vision Quest yourself?" I asked.

"Yes. It changed my life." he responded. "While most of us live in a man-made world, we also know that we have a special connection to nature. You can see this when folks want to go on camping trips, to go to beautiful natural settings like our national parks, or just want to be outside. You were just at Yellowstone with your son. How did that make you feel when you were there?"

I smiled, as I thought of the crowds in Yellowstone,

"It made me feel like there were a lot of people on their own searches." My smile faded as I continued, "Honestly, though, I think we're all drawn to these places for a reason. I think we have an inherent need to connect with nature."

"Exactly," he responded. "We do have a need for nature. It's because nature connects us to the Great Spirit, the one my people call Waken Tanka. My people see God in all of nature. We believe that by respecting the natural world, we are brought closer to God. I believe there is a certain lack of integrity, something very superficial, about living in the man-made world of concrete, skyscrapers and pollution. We need nature, not just to balance our lives, but also to re-energize us at a spiritual level. The plants and trees around this cabin were planted here with love and appreciation for what they give to the place. They have flourished because of love and appreciation given to them. I appreciate them, and they give me something back. Love and appreciation go a long way, Coach," he said, smiling. "I wanted to feel closer to the Great Spirit. This place does that for me. It's a simple, but fulfilling existence up here. I generate my own electricity when I need it at all. I also have the water I need. I take care of the place and respect it and the plant life here. It's a peaceful coexistence. As you can see, there is no TV or computer here. It is really a pretty simple existence."

"I think it's that simplicity that is most attractive to me," I said. "It just feels right here."

"That was my primary motivation for building this place." he responded. "Keep it simple, build with quality and respect the earth around it."

"This would definitely be quality," I said.

Great Thunder nodded as he looked at me and said,

"The 'quality' thing is very important to understand. I knew that for me to do justice to the environment, my work had to be the best I was capable of. Otherwise, this house would be a slap in the face to the Great Spirit and disrespectful of the natural surroundings." He was quiet for a moment, before asking, "How would you define the word quality?"

I chewed on a large bite of the best apple pie I had ever eaten, wondering if my answer could do justice to the question. Unsure of myself, I finally responded,

"I think quality can be defined from both internal and external perspectives. If we use our own judgment and common sense, we decide on our own if something is of quality. I think we define quality based on our experiences. The more experiences we have, the more information we have to define quality." Then, I paused, "I don't think that's how most of us operate, though."

"How's that?" he asked.

I went on, "I'm guessing that we most often determine quality from the outside. What I mean is that quality is often determined by a consensus, a majority opinion, if you will. The bottom line is that we listen to others to get information we need, especially approval."

Great Thunder interjected, "So, what if a large group looks at a modern abstract painting? Would you say that some might see it as a great piece of art, some might think it as awful, and others still might be clueless and would reserve judgment until others might first give them some guidance?"

"I guess all of that is correct," I responded carefully. "I think I see your point. Some might wait to determine the quality of the painting after reading an art critic or listening to the opinions of others."

Great Thunder stood up and walked to the door.

"Coach, come out to the porch." Surveying the incredible view and sweeping his arm across the horizon, he asked, "Would this be quality?"

"It would certainly be beauty," I responded, with a smile. "But I'm not sure folks would understand it in the context of quality, even though I would say it's of the highest quality.

Let the Learning Begin

My guess is that most people define quality as a sort of rating, a rating often linked to what others think."

"Yes, I expect you're right," said Great Thunder. "Quality should be the goal of all people: quality in the way we live our lives, our productivity, our parenting, our work. Building this small cabin to the highest level of my abilities gave me great pleasure. What is most interesting is that, because I did my best, it fits here and it has made for a better connection with the Great Spirit. As well, doing it right has made me stronger as a person." He paused for a few seconds before asking,

"Have you ever done something that, in retrospect, was the very best you could do?"

I thought long and hard for something, but could not answer in the affirmative.

"I guess we all fall short to some extent, in everything we try to do."

"Yes, we do," he replied. He swung his arm across the horizon, saying, "This is quality. Nothing man-made will ever match this."

After a few moments of appreciating the view, he said,

"Coach, quality must be defined by each of us, from the inside-out. Tell me, what is it like being in a line of work where success is based on competition, where one's worth is based on a comparison with others?"

I thought for a moment, and then began,

"Well, competition has its good side and its bad. When it's done in a healthy manner, it can be terrific."

"And what is that healthy manner?" he asked.

I responded, "Healthy competition with another means that both parties are working together, using each other, if you will, to get to a higher level of performance. When it's done right, I think it can get us to our best performance. I'm not sure that our highest level of performance can be attained without some level of competition."

Great Thunder responded, "Interesting. I don't think we'll ever get rid of competition in our society or even in the world. 'Survival of the fittest' is the purest form of competition. It thrives today just as it did thousands of years ago, just in a more socially acceptable manner. Of course, it's also the root of stratification in this society. Those with the money and the power will make every effort to stay in power. My people could not compete with the money and military power of the white man during the westward movement. Like so many other cultures in past, it was assimilation or annihilation. Of course, to some degree, both happened to the American Indian."

I sat quietly, as Great Thunder continued, "You're right, Coach. Competition can be good. Unfortunately, it often is not. There's a dark side. When our goal is to defeat another, and only that, we lose a part of our soul in the process. And that is my concern. What will we give up at the soul level, in the process of besting another? I believe the cost is often greater than the return."

"But we like to be challenged, don't we, regardless of culture?" I asked. "And competition provides that in spades."

"Of course," he replied. "It's the one thread that all people of all cultures share. We all want to be better at what we do and we all want to improve our place in this world, and that of our children. Unfortunately, many will do whatever it takes, including acting immorally or unethically, to improve their stock in life. I really enjoyed my time with the rodeo because it was about me and the horse, or me and the bull, one-on-one. The animal's goal was to get me off his back as fast as possible. My goal was to do what I had to do to stay on him for eight seconds. It was an interesting and intense dance between us, with my moves countering what he offered. I lost the contest more times than I won. But the challenge kept bringing me back. I loved the thrill of the competition. And, I always had a great deal of respect for the animals."

We sat quietly for a few moments, when he said,

"One of the reasons you are here is to understand how your many experiences have shaped you, so you can teach your athletes in a manner that is healthy and productive. The learning experiences we have are many. The truth is, we miss most of them when they happen, often considering them to be just mundane everyday occurrences. Of course, it's these everyday life experiences that hold the greatest potential for learning. All experiences are important, no matter how big, small, good or bad. The truth is, most of our meaningful learning experiences come from our failures."

I nodded. I had certainly lived this truth myself as a young coach.

He went on, "You know, life is like the waves of the ocean with its non-stop highs and lows. Life, too, has highs and lows. Most people do their best to dismiss the lows because they are painful or difficult. We don't like unhappiness, disappointment, failure and pain. However, we need to pay special attention to the meaning of all of these experiences. We have to remember that our lives will always have highs and lows. It's a fact of life. I've learned to see the negative events in my life as being there for a reason. To understand those reasons, I must first accept the negative events. We have to face the fact that bad things do happen to good people. Our challenge is to figure out how we can grow from all of our experiences, good and bad. One of the biggest challenges your students will face, like all young people, is learning to deal with selfishness. Manipulation is a very powerful tool further developed as the child grows and learns more about the environment and his place in it. Through social learning, we learn that our society places a high demand on social comparison and competition with others. It's easy to see why many folks have problems as they get older. Our self-worth is often tied to how we compare ourselves to others."

I told Great Thunder that I was very interested in the difference between the inner self and the outer self.

"Yes," he responded, "there is often quite a conflict between the two selves. We can rationalize and justify, but we cannot lie to ourselves at a core level. The outer world will shape our souls if we let it. Most of the time, we aren't even aware of it happening. Not only can we be shaped from the outside, our souls can be ruled from the outside. We see so many examples of this. We are most often defined by what we own, whom we know and what we have accomplished, all of which are externally driven. Many folks are more than happy to sell their souls for fame and fortune. But those things I mentioned will get them no closer to finding themselves or to finding happiness."

I smiled and said, "I guess that is why I am here, to get closer to finding out who I am."

Great Thunder nodded in affirmation, then continued,

"The inner self is where we find truth, peace and acceptance. Of course we must first recognize our inner self. Many people are so caught up in their externally-driven lives that they are incapable of defining themselves from the inside. They continually let others define them ... mostly out of habit. It's a sad, but true commentary that we often see ourselves only as others see us. Seems to me we should know best our own abilities and worth, don't you think?"

He picked up the plates and cups from the porch and added,

"Feel free to sit out here and enjoy the vista. I'll take care of these and be back out in a while."

I sat on the porch and surveyed the incredible view, thinking to myself how much my sense of self-worth was defined by others: the performance of my teams, the quality of things I had written, even my days as an athlete.

My days as an athlete ... I was one mixed-up kid back then. After finishing a successful collegiate career as a pole-vaulter at the University of Florida, I felt lost. While I had a degree, I thought of myself first and foremost as an athlete. Pole vaulting was the most important thing in the world to me, mainly because it was the thing I did the best. I smiled as I remembered how my worthiness as a person was measured by my ability to fly through the air on a fiberglass tube.

I thought of the time when I first began to wonder about a future after pole vaulting. In the summer of 1978, I had been out of school a couple of years and had been to Europe to compete. I had met my future wife, fallen in love and had begun to think seriously about what lay ahead. I was scared to death of the prospects. I had made the decision to move to Canada while my future wife finished her second degree at the University of Toronto. She was one of Canada's top high jumpers, and I would train full-time under her coach. It was an interesting year as I trained more than six hours per day. I was never faster, stronger, or more physically fit. Yet I was vaulting poorly. I couldn't understand how I could be doing so much quality training and not be performing better than I was. I became so frustrated that I chose to take that outdoor season off to try to figure out if I still wanted to continue in the sport. After making the finals of the Olympic trials in 1976, but failing to make the Olympic team, I had made the decision to stick it out for four more years to try to make the team in 1980. I wasn't sure I'd continue till 1980.

The year 1979 brought many changes in my life. In the summer of that year, my wife and I were married in Canada. As well, I was offered an assistantship in the graduate studies program in biomechanics at Indiana University, Bloomington. The intensive 12-month master's program would mean that I would be teaching five courses while taking another five of my own at the same time ... and I would be doing this while training to make the 1980 Olympic team. I would have to do it with the vault being a fourth priority behind my new marriage, going to school and teaching my students.

Let the Learning Begin

With an incredibly difficult schedule and with only one hour each day to train, I had the best year of my vaulting career. It was an amazing lesson to me, and helped to put the vaulting in perspective. While it was a wonderful final season, I again failed to make the Olympic team. Of course those Trials were an exercise in futility. The United States would not be attending the Games of Moscow. The American boycott of the 1980 Games was a painful realization that sports and politics are forever intertwined. Those Olympic Trials were the end of it for me. I left my poles on the track that day in Eugene, walking away from the sport that had defined me as a person. It was time to move on, and as scary as the prospect of life without the vault was, we at least had coaching jobs in place for us in Iowa.

I had finished my master's degree, vaulted at the Olympic Trials, turned in my final thesis paper and drove to Grinnell, Iowa all in the space of two weeks. No longer an athlete, I would now be defined as a coach. I knew nothing about coaching, and it showed. I would take some hard falls along the way, but eventually would find success in coaching. Getting a handle on my inner self, however, would take a bit longer.

Great Thunder came back outside with a cup of fresh tea for me.

"Do you want to see something that will touch your soul?" he asked.

"Sure, I replied."

"Then, plan to stay the night up here. I'll make a nice spot for you to sleep out under the stars. It will be a show like you've never seen before. I've got plenty of blankets."

Before I could resist, he added, "I think you need to do this, Coach. I'll get things set up for you later. Why don't you ride down to your motel and get your stuff. It seems a waste of money to be paying for a room. This will save you a couple of night's charges. You'll be picking Cameron up the day after tomorrow. You can stay up here and camp out both nights. It will be good for your soul to be out of the rat race for a couple of days. I think sleeping outside on the land is a way for you to connect with the earth, and to God."

I thought it over, and agreed.

"Thank you very much. Again, how will I repay you?"

"As I said before, you will repay me by teaching others about what you learn."

"And I expect I have plenty to learn," I responded with a smile.

"We'll see," he said.

I rode the bike down to Cody, deep in thought all the way. I checked out of the motel and gave the lady at the desk my cell number just in case Cameron called the motel. I also left a message at the dude ranch, letting them know to get a hold of me. It was also a chance for me to covertly check on him. The desk attendant at the ranch assured me he was doing great, something that made me feel better about leaving him there alone.

When I arrived back at the cabin, I could smell something wonderful cooking. I could see that the blankets were already outside and ready for me. As I knocked on the screen door, Great Thunder welcomed me again. "Come on in Coach, I hope you're hungry."

"Come to think of it, I am," I replied. My mind has been so busy thinking about other things that I had forgotten that the only food I've all day was a piece of apple pie. "Smells great! What's cooking?"

"An old favorite" he said. "Good food for thinking," he said, smiling.

As we feasted on a delicious homemade burrito casserole, Great Thunder told me about the process of beseeching, the Native American form of prayer to the Great Spirit. He also told me of how the gift of tobacco was a common form of expression as a gift to both the Great Spirit and to those who practice the medicine. "You will need to know these things," he said. He gave me a small packet of loose tobacco, saying,

"It's good to have this with you. You never know when a good prayer is in order. You simply sprinkle some of it around, or, if seeking help from one who offers medicine, offer it as a gift."

I thanked him, now knowing there was no turning back on this path I had taken. The die had been cast, and I was moving forward, still a bit disconcerted about where all this was leading, but also excited about it all.

After the tasty dinner, we moved to the porch, coffee in hand.

"Unfortunately, I will need to be leaving town tomorrow," Great Thunder said. "A friend's family in South Dakota needs my medicine, and I will likely be with them for a few days. I want you to feel free to stay here until you need to leave. Bring Cameron up here if you would like. I usually leave the back door unlocked."

"Aren't you afraid of someone breaking in?" I asked.

"No" he said. "No one really knows of this place. If they do come upon it, I want it to be available to them if they need it." I nodded in agreement, seeing why this man had been chosen to help others.

That evening, as I lay under the most beautiful starlit sky I had ever seen, I wondered what else I would discover about myself on this trip. I decided to sprinkle some tobacco around the makeshift bed of blankets and I prayed to God for guidance as I dealt with questions about meaning in my life. While I could hear coyotes and other animals in the distance, I had no fear of sleeping in such an idyllic and quiet place. The cool, dry air and the slight breeze brought me to a deep sleep.

I had the most amazing dream that night. In it, I was communicating directly with animals. I remember speaking to an eagle, a chameleon and a deer just as if I were speaking with another human. It was the most amazing, clear dream I have ever had. I awoke with a start in the middle of the night and quickly grabbed my journal. Using the full moon, I was able to write down what I had seen in the dream. I had been camping in a canyon. I could actually talk with the animals, which showed no fear of me. They spoke as if they were teachers, telling me to recognize that all animals were capable of communicating. I felt no fear of them, only great interest in what they were saying to me. I had trouble getting back to sleep, still amazed by the intensity and clarity of the dream.

I awoke at daylight and checked my watch: 6:15. I sat up and tried to recall everything I could about the dream.

"Hey, sleepyhead!" I turned to see Great Thunder walking out the door with coffee cups in hand. I stood up and stretched before taking a cup.

"Thanks." I said, "Man, what a dream I had."

When I told him the details, he responded,

"This is good! You need to try to remember your dreams. Write them down. Dreams tell us plenty about ourselves and even about our future ... if we reflect and try to make sense of them."

"What do you think it meant, that I could actually communicate with the animals?" I asked.

"There's no surprise in that. We can all connect with animals, perhaps most clearly in our dreams. Each of these animals was trying to tell you something. When our young folks go out on a Vision Quest experience, they often have these kinds of dreams, with intense connections to animals. The types of animals you dream about can also tell you plenty. Tell me more about the dream."

I thought for a moment and began,

"I was in some sort of canyon. It was beautiful, with lush vegetation, a small river and lots of animals walking about. It was serene. I felt totally at peace and I remember communicating with the animals. I did more listening than talking. There was some strange form of connection going on. It was more than just talking ... it was like I could feel what they were feeling."

"And what animals were there?" he asked.

"I remember a deer, a chameleon and an eagle ... actually there were several eagles, three, I think. I do remember connecting with each of them. I think there were other animals ... they were certainly around, but I only remember directly communicating with the deer, chameleon and eagles." He nodded as I spoke.

"Do you remember anything specific about your interaction with the animals?" he asked.

"Not really, I just felt at peace with them. There was no fear in either direction. They were talking to me, but not in the ordinary sense. Again, it was like I could feel what they were feeling."

I listened intently as Great Thunder told me about each of the three animals, and their meaning.

"The chameleon can change colors from green to brown. Do you recall its color?"

"Yes," I replied. "It was a green color. I wrote it down in my journal. It would just sit near me, as if it had something to share."

"That's good. Green is its happy color. It appears it was comfortable with you. Chameleons are very sensitive to the environment, and this one could trust you and feel what you were about. This is a sign of your intuitive powers being awakened. This is good. Tell me about the doe."

"It came right up to me and looked me in the eye. I don't remember any specifics about what it told me."

Great Thunder nodded, and said, "The deer is a sign of growth and expansion of your psyche. It's a sign of opportunity for you ... and a sign of new growth in you. And you said there were eagles? Tell me how you encountered them in your dream."

"Well, there was more than one ... three, in fact. They were flying in formation above me, where they seemed to stay even as I changed position."

Great Thunder thought for a moment and said,

"The eagle is an animal of creativity and spirituality. It's an animal to help you rediscover your lost self, the self you had at your birth. The eagle is considered a messenger from heaven. It will help you to awaken a higher sense of purpose and purity. That you saw three of them is important. Three is the number of new birth and creativity. Coach, this isn't just about you finding yourself. It is about awakening an ability in you to teach others."

"Wow, I'm amazed at all of this," I said. "I'm still not sure what to make of it all."

"That's why you're here." he responded, matter-of-factly. "Cameron is finding out things about himself where he is. The lessons are many in our lives. They occur at different times, and at different levels of intensity. It's important that we recognize that all things that happen to us occur for a reason. There are lessons in all of it."

"I understand, I think. I'm still trying to process it all." I sat quietly for a few moments before asking, "Did you really know I was coming to Cody?"

"Yes," he responded. "I knew that I would be meeting with another teacher who would be seeking me out. It takes two people to create a connection like this. You were looking for something that I could provide. I knew that I was called to help illuminate some things for you, things that you are fully capable of understanding when you can see them."

I let that sink in as I sipped the coffee.

"What time do you leave today?" I asked.

"Right now, unfortunately," he replied. "We will not see each other for a while, but we will see each other again, of that I am sure. I wrote you a note. It's on the table inside. Give some thought to what's in it. You need to know that you are in the teaching profession for a reason. Continue to grow, my friend. There is plenty wrong with this world, but few things that can't be fixed with education and the recognition of truth. You were called here for a reason. Never doubt that."

With that, he extended his hand. I gave him a firm, appreciative handshake and walked with him to his pickup. As he opened the door and threw a small bag in the rear, he said,

"Come back anytime. If the place is locked, there's a key under the big white rock out back. Please give my best to your son. He seems like a very fine boy." He looked right through me as he said, "We will meet again. Don't fear what is ahead, Coach."

"Wait a second," I said. "How will I get in touch with you?"

"We will meet again when we're supposed to, down the road. But first you need to travel some of that road." With a final smile and a wave, he yelled,

"Goodbye, Coach," and got into the truck.

I sat quietly watching the pickup drive away, still trying to digest everything, the conversations with Great Thunder, the dream, and the purpose of our turning north on this trip. He knew I was coming, I thought to myself. What did he mean by 'Don't fear what is ahead'?

Let the Learning Begin

I got up and walked into the cabin and looked for the note on the table. It was in a plain white envelope with "Coach" written on it. I opened it and began reading,

Dear Coach,

Like myself, you are a teacher. You've been called to this honored profession. Like all of us, you have special gifts. You are fortunate that you work with so many talented young people, young people who are looking for mentorship and direction in this difficult world. You have been chosen to understand things at a deeper level, so you can teach them things that matter. My job is to simply help get you started on the path to this knowledge of the world and your place in it.

-These are some things that might help:
-Listen to intuition. We all have spirit helpers (many call them guardian angels) that aid us in the challenges of our lives. Yours are looking after you, but you must listen to your intuition to hear them.
-Try to understand your dreams. We dream for a reason. Often, dreams can show us our path and what is right. Try to remember them. You might want to have a pad of paper by your sleeping place. Write about your dreams as soon as you awaken. There will be plenty of time later to reflect on them.
-Show integrity in all that you do. Live with quality, honesty and integrity in your work and life. It makes a difference to those you teach.
-God is everywhere: in every rock, tree, blade of grass and every animal. Respect them, and they will help guide you when needed. The natural world has been good to us and has always provided us with what we've needed. Things that go against natural harmony and balance must be recognized and changed.

-Simplify your life. "Things" get in the way of our growth. You already know this. Try living without accumulating things. It will make the things that actually matter in life incredibly important to you.

-Find time for solitude, to think without outside interference. This will be important to you. It will require you to get over the fear of being alone. This fear is something all people feel. Only the strong have learned how to be alone and to enjoy what solitude can offer. It is necessary for us to grow spiritually.

-You shape your own spirit with the choices you make every day. When we make choices that are wrong, we will ultimately have to pay for them, both in this life and in the afterlife. Most religions share this belief. When not sure about a choice, pray ... then trust your intuition.

-Seek wisdom, not just knowledge. Books give us knowledge. Only life experiences can give us wisdom. Knowledge is about the past, wisdom about the future. You have the potential for great wisdom, but you must first live more of life's experiences.

-Pray for guidance. As I mentioned to you earlier, you will do a Vision Quest. It won't happen for a while, but you'll know when it's time. In the Quest you will beseech the Great Spirit for meaning to your life. As I have told you, it helps when you are beseeching to offer a gift to the creator. I suggest loose tobacco. I've left some with this note. Scatter it around the places you pray, reflect or write. It will be well received if you pray with an open heart and ask for guidance in the process.

-Find ways to be in nature. There is an old Lakota saying, 'When man moves away from nature, his heart becomes hard.' Nature can help you find yourself.

-Finally, never be afraid to face your fears. It is the facing of fears that builds courage. We are not born with courage, it must be learned.

Coach, you came north on your trip because we were supposed to meet. My job is to plant seeds within you. Now you must work on growing

Let the Learning Begin

these seeds. Listen to and trust your dreams and your intuition. Your spirit helpers are there for you. Respect the earth and keep learning about yourself and nature. You must continue your spiritual journey.

We will meet again. First, you need some time for some experiences to occur. They will be your "on-the-job" training. There is work to do. I will know when you are ready to meet again. You, too, will know. At that time, we will re-connect. Find your heart on this journey. And remember, your first teacher is your own heart. All the best to you on your path until we meet again,

Great Thunder

I sat at the table and re-read the letter slowly, trying to digest it all. Why is this happening to me, I wondered? I thought of everything that had happened in the three days since arriving in Cody. I pulled out my journal and went back outside on the porch. I sat for a while, not knowing how to start writing, and finally closed the journal and stared at the gorgeous view. I'm not sure where this whole thing will take me, I thought, but I may not get another chance at this. I resolved to accept what was happening and not try too hard to make sense of it all.

I read the letter many times that day, wondering what the next step would be. All I knew for sure was that I would be doing a Vision Quest at some point. I rode down into Cody for dinner at the Irma. It was a quiet time of reflection. After eating, I walked down the main strip, looking into the windows of the many shops, but my thoughts were far away. I wanted to get back up the mountain.

After riding back to the cabin that evening, I felt emotionally drained as I again lay on the blankets under the night sky. The stars seemed even brighter than the night before. I was beginning to like this idea of sleeping outdoors, connecting to the earth. Perhaps my subconscious brain, and perhaps a higher order, knew that I could take no more heavy thinking, or dreams. I had a deep and relaxing sleep and awoke to the most amazing, colorful sunrise in front of me. I felt re-energized and excited about the prospects for the future. I needed to pick up Cameron at 4:00, so I cleaned myself up, filled a large bucket with water from the brook, washed and packed the bike in preparation for the ride home to Iowa.

Before leaving Great Thunder's cabin, I cleaned things up and wrote him a note thanking him for his time, his honesty and his positive energy. I made a point of sprinkling tobacco around the cabin, giving thanks for both the place and the man. Before mounting up I sprinkled some around the bike, praying for safety on the ride home. I also asked for guidance in understanding the deeper meaning of this trip. With a final look back at Great Thunder's beautiful cabin, I fired up the big motor and headed slowly down the gravel drive, back to the road toward Cody. While I wished I didn't have to leave so soon, I felt a renewed energy and purpose as I rode, ready for whatever the future held.

Back in Cody, I found a coffee shop where I would try to write down the special events of the past two days. Several hours later, cramps in my hand told me it was time to stop. I mounted the bike and found the road that led to the Ranch where Cameron was having his own special experience. I smiled to myself, thinking about how, just a few days earlier,

Let the Learning Begin

we were headed to California on a very different path. How quickly things can change. After weeks of preparation to visit L.A., we had changed our path after watching a movie in Denver. Yes, intuition is a powerful thing ... and I'm glad we'd listened.

I pulled up to the main ranch house a couple of minutes early and could see that Cameron was already waiting outside with some new friends. He bounded over to the bike, bursting with energy,

"Dad, you won't believe it! I learned how to ride a horse and rope cows! I even helped with branding this morning!"

His face was beaming with excitement and a newfound confidence in himself.

"It was incredible! We slept outside last night. You should have seen the stars. There were so many!"

I decided not to tell him about my experience, wanting this to be his moment.

"So, what kind of horse did you ride?"

"I'm not sure, but I think it was a mare. I didn't fall off even once. Dad, it was amazing! I want to do this again sometime, maybe for a whole summer!"

I felt wonderful, knowing Cameron had enjoyed a special learning experience that he would forever remember. He brought his friends over to show them the bike, and I left them alone as I went inside to pay the bill. It gave him a chance to say goodbye to both the staff and his new young friends who had joined him for the past two days. I could tell that he felt a special feeling for one of the cowboys on the staff. I couldn't hear what he said to the man, but the cowboy tousled his hair after he shook his hand.

"You take care, Cameron," said the man, as my oldest walked back toward me.

"I will. I'll try to get back again." The cowboy tipped his hat to me, saying with a smile, "He's a good boy."

I nodded to the cowboy and voiced a quiet "thank you" to him as I passed. The moment had me thinking about how much of an influence an adult can have on a young person. I loaded Cameron's gear, using elastic cords to tie his new cowboy hat onto the top of the bags. Finally ready, Cameron gave a last wave to his new friends and we started out of the parking lot toward the road home.

"Back on the road, again, Cam!" I yelled over my shoulder.

"Yup! Dad, this was the best thing I have ever done. Thanks!" he yelled back as he squeezed me.

"Glad you liked it, Bud. How about we see a little of Montana before we head back east?"

"Sounds good to me!"

I made a mental note to try to look into possible horseback rides for the kids back in Iowa.

We rode the bike to Bozeman and spent a relaxing day and night in the college town, before riding east into the mountains south of Livingston to see the ranch used in *The Horse Whisperer*, the movie that had motivated the change in our trip. We stopped the bike near the entrance to the ranch used in the movie, surveying the amazing view in all directions. This truly was Big Sky Country, with a beauty all its own. It was easy to see why Robert Redford has picked this location for the movie. We pointed the bike east, later making

Let the Learning Begin

a stop at the Little Big Horn, the site of the 1876 battle where George Custer and 287 other soldiers were annihilated by Sioux and Cheyenne warriors. That battle, perhaps more than any other of that period, shocked White Americans. It did little to stop the Westward movement.

We spent a couple of days in the Black Hills before the final push home. After the requisite visit to Mount Rushmore, we made a stop at the Crazy Horse Memorial, dedicated to the great Oglala Lakota warrior and leader. I was surprised at the impact it had on me. Crazy Horse became infamous as the conqueror of George Custer at the Little Bighorn. Known for his humility and bravery, he was deeply respected and loved by his people. He would be the last Lakota leader to surrender to the United States government. The sheer size of the memorial, one that will eventually dwarf the Presidents at Mount Rushmore, spoke to both of us. As we walked up to the base of the Crazy Horse monument, I quietly offered up some tobacco, praying for all Native Americans, and asking forgiveness for what those before me had done to them. The white man's movement westward had swallowed up the Native American population and its culture. It was justified as progress. I hoped the monument would be finished in my lifetime. I had a feeling I would be back here in the future.

As we mounted the bike to leave the Black Hills, I knew that I would not be returning to Iowa the same person. I hoped I would not fall back into the same life as before.

It was a long day on the saddle from the Black Hills to Iowa. Exhausted, both physically and emotionally, it took a few days to recover from the experience. I was still trying to get my head around the greater meaning of what had happened on our trip when the girls returned from Holland.

My eight-year old daughter Deidre, upon hearing about Cameron's experience, asked, "Daddy, will I be able to go on a motorcycle trip like this someday?"

"You bet, Deidre," I said. "When you're eleven or twelve, we'll do a trip just like Cameron's."

As hard as I tried, it wasn't long before I began to fall back into the habits and realities of my former life. As I often tell my athletes, 'Repetition is the mother of learning'. And so, too, it is with our lives. The bike trip and the meaning of the talks with Great Thunder became increasingly distant memories. Now and then, I would think about the trip and the wise Indian, wondering if we would ever meet again.

I hoped so.

Part Three

The Quest

Listen to the voice of nature, for it holds treasures for you.
Huron Indian Saying

*T*wo years after my special bike trip with Cameron, both my wife and I were up for a sabbatical leave. We took our family along for four months to Nassau, Bahamas. The head of the ruling body for Bahamian Track and Field, and a graduate of Grinnell College, had asked us to come down and train coaches and athletes. We left Iowa in December and stayed until late March, missing the indoor track season back home. One of the most valuable aspects of the trip was enrolling our kids as students at a large school where they were three of only a handful of white children. They would experience what it meant to be a minority. It was important to me that they, too, began to see the big picture.

When I was not teaching coaches or working with athletes, I devoted my time to writing about what had happened on the bike trip two years previous. I had struck up a friendship with the owner of the Cricket Club in Nassau, and was offered a special outdoor table with a beautiful view of the ocean where I could work. I would walk each day to the

Club, looking forward to writing. It was this process that helped me to renew the many feelings I had experienced on the bike trip with Cameron. The writing also prompted something I didn't expect.

I began to have dreams --- powerful, lucid dreams with Native American themes. It was in one of these dreams that I had a conversation with a very old Native American wise man. I was seated in a circle with several Native men inside a small hut. I could tell that the others had great respect for the Old One. I knew I was there to ask him for answers. When I did, he spoke to me very quietly, very matter-of-factly, "I have no answers for you. You must find the answers." We sat quietly for a while, and he continued, "You are to do a Vision Quest. It will occur soon. It will be in the Chaco Canyon area and it will be done when the sun is at its highest place in the sky. You must prepare yourself for this. Do not deny yourself this experience. It is something you must do."

I awoke from the dream with a start, immediately writing down everything I could remember on a pad I kept on the bedside table. I knew that this was the message that Great Thunder had told me I would one day receive. I would do a Vision Quest in the Chaco Canyon area ... wherever that was. This whole thing was getting a bit crazy!

By the time we returned to the States, I had already begun doing homework on Vision Quests and the Chaco Canyon area (land of the Ancient Ones, the Anasazi), which I learned was in Northern New Mexico. I searched on the internet and found a number of Vision Quest options offered around the country, including one in New Mexico. I copied the materials on several, and laid them out on the dining room table. I would let my intuition help me choose.

The paperwork for the New Mexico Quest kept drawing me to it. Finally, I called the number listed and spoke with a man named Jack. He was planning a Vision Quest for that summer for a select number of participants. I had a lot of questions, and we talked for some time about the Vision Quest and its meaning. He recommended that I pray about it in order to find out if this was the right thing for me to do and if he was the one to lead me on that journey. At the end of our talk, he requested a written letter of my purpose and intention. After several days of considering the location and Jack as the leader, I was convinced it was the right choice. I called him back, set up the arrangements, and mailed my letter of intention. He explained that the group would be together to receive a couple of days of instruction before separating for five days and four nights of being alone in the wilderness.

I would be riding my motorcycle to New Mexico and then leave the bike in Santa Fe while on the Quest. I asked Jack if I could leave the cycle at his place, to which he agreed. After completing the Quest, I would ride south to pick up Deidre at the Albuquerque airport. She would get her wish to follow in Cameron's footsteps and have her own bike trip with her dad. While Cameron and I never made it to California on our bike trip, Deidre and I would.

Upon our return to Iowa from the Bahamas, we finished the spring semester with a successful outdoor track season. It was good to be home again. Teaching, coaching and recruiting in the spring semester had always been challenging, with so much to do and too few hours to do it. Still, I would often find myself daydreaming about the Quest that was ahead.

My daughter and I began planning in earnest for the second motorcycle trip. After the Quest, we would ride from New Mexico, through Arizona, and on to L.A. to visit friends in Santa Monica. We then would ride across Nevada, Utah, Colorado and Kansas before returning home. The Quest would begin in the second week of July. While I was excited about the trip, I also began to feel an unexplained sense of fear. Initially writing it off as a normal response to the risks of another bike trip, I began to pay attention to it as the sense of foreboding increased. I wasn't sure of the source, but it was definitely a feeling of fear, and it was becoming almost palpable as the trip approached.

Finally, departure day arrived. I had packed the bike the night before, still feeling an unexplainable tension about the trip. I prayed about it before going to sleep, hoping I would feel better in the morning. After an early breakfast, I kissed my wife and kids and pulled out of our driveway. As I gunned the motor and began another two-wheeled adventure, I yelled, "I'll see you in a week and a half in Albuquerque, Deidre."

I wasn't even a mile from the house when I asked myself, "Why am I doing this? What am I trying to prove, and to whom?" Tears filled my eyes and I had to pull over for a moment to collect myself. I was committed now. Deidre's ticket had been bought, our friends in California were expecting us, and I had made a commitment to Jack in New Mexico. This trip was a go, regardless of fears.

The Quest

The big 6-cylinder Honda of the previous trip had been sold. I now motored along on a smaller, but equally powerful BMW road bike. The bike was made for this kind of riding, and flowed along Interstate 35 south to Kansas City. I rode comfortably at seventy-five miles per hour, with it feeling more like fifty-five. I stopped for a quick brunch just north of KC at a Waffle House ... one of my favorite places to eat when I was in school at the University of Florida. It was a rare site in the Midwest, and I took advantage of it. After eating and filling the bike's tank as well, I continued south on I-35 toward Emporia. It was there that I moved onto State Road 50. I was now headed west on the two-lane highways that I preferred. It was still early in the day, but it was already hot.

I stopped for gas in Hutchinson, still unable to escape the unexplainable feeling of dread. That, along with the increasing heat, was about to get the best of me. I was continually checking the air temperature gauge on the dashboard of the bike as it continued climbing: 103, 104, 106, 109 degrees. I wasn't sure how much this bike could take. Knowing the motor was water cooled, I figured it could handle just about any temperature. But I began to wonder about the tires. How hot could they get before becoming a safety issue? I also wondered how much heat I could handle. I was now stopping at virtually every small town to take on water and to escape for a few moments into air conditioning. With every stop, it took all the courage I could muster to not turn the bike around. What was I was afraid of?

I remembered Great Thunder's charge to have courage and face my fears. So this is how courage is built, I thought? Well, I'm not exactly having fun with this.

I'd long since closed the vents on the big windshield. The air coming through them felt like a hot blow dryer on its high setting. I decided to make it to Dodge City and then call it a day. I'm glad I did. Too drained to set up the tent, I checked into a small roadside motor court motel. Thankfully, the room was clean and had a working air conditioner. I turned it on full, shed my gear and chugged a large bottle of Gatorade. After a short nap, I took the bike into town to find a carwash to get the bugs off the big windshield. Cleaning the bike took more energy than I thought it should, evidence of how much the hot ride had taken out of me. I returned to the room and parked the bike under the small porch outside my door, glad to finally be off the saddle. It had been a long, hard day of riding. I only hoped it would get easier.

I took a welcome cool shower and walked into the Old Town section of Dodge City, preserved to look just like the old West. A short walk up to Boot Hill Cemetery (the first in the U.S.) made me think of just how short life could be 120 years ago. Named because most were buried with their boots on, I saw few gravestones of people who had lived beyond twenty-five years of age. What challenges had these folks faced? It had to have been a touch and go life. What had they learned in their short time on earth? As I stood looking at the many gravestones, I had the feeling that something in me, too, was going to die on this trip. I prayed that I would get home safe and sound.

After sitting on the porch of the motel and watching an amazing show of heat lightning that night, I finally crashed and fell into a deep sleep, beaten down by both the long, hot ride and my apprehensions about the trip. I was too tired to write much in my journal:

> "Day One ... not much fun. Hot as hell.
> I'm afraid of something. The frustrating part is that I don't know what it is.
> It's the first day and I feel like I've been through a tornado. I hope things get better."

The next morning was better. I felt rejuvenated after a night of air conditioning. The morning broke cool and clear as I started for New Mexico. I stayed on Highway 56 South and left Kansas for a quick jaunt through the Northwest tip of Oklahoma. From there, I was quickly into New Mexico where I stopped for a late breakfast and gas in Clayton. Next came a smooth and beautiful ride to Springer, where I had to jump onto I-25 for a few short miles north. I exited onto Colorado 58, the road that would take me from Cimarron to Taos New Mexico, a place I had always wanted to visit. The beautiful ride was over too soon. With a spare day in hand, I decided to spend the day and night in Taos, a place known for its mixture of skiers, outdoor types and spiritual seekers. I felt comfortable as I walked through the streets marveling at the many small, unique shops. This is a place where I could end up, I thought to myself. I need to come back here some day and spend more time.

The bike was running perfectly and I was feeling better about the trip. After finding a place to set up my tent just outside of Taos in Shady Brook, I built a small fire and pulled out the letter that Great Thunder had left me two years earlier at his cabin. *"Find Solitude,"* he had written.

Well, I'm finding that on this trip, I thought. I had never felt so alone. Maybe that was the real purpose of this trip. I knew I needed to learn to live with myself, to accept myself, before I could offer something to others.

It was a quiet night. I lay in my sleeping bag thinking about how this trip had began; still worried that something wasn't totally right about all of it. Maybe it was how unsure I was about the whole Vision Quest experience. I hoped I was strong enough to face my concerns with courage. I prayed for that courage and finally, tired of thinking, fell into a deep sleep.

I awoke refreshed and rode into Taos for a quick breakfast. Finding a coffee shop where I could sit outside on a deck that opened onto a beautiful flower garden, I sat there and an extraordinary thing occurred. I had ordered my food and was sitting quietly, appreciating the garden, when a very large Monarch butterfly landed on my shirtsleeve. I held my arm steady and stared at it, just inches away from my face. It was staring back at me. After a good thirty seconds, I won the stare-down and it flew off. I smiled at the symbolism of the moment, thinking about the metamorphosis that the caterpillar had gone through to become such a beautiful butterfly. I expected that I, too, would likely be shedding some of my old self for something new on this trip.

"Want to join us tonight?" I was jarred out of my thoughts by a pretty lady of about forty, passing out leaflets. She was dressed in a beautiful, multi-colored cotton skirt, white top and Birkenstocks on her feet. "Sorry, I didn't mean to interrupt your thoughts," she said with a sweet smile. She handed me a leaflet.

"No, not at all. What have you got here?" I asked, as I took the flyer from her hand.

"We're having a seminar tonight on Soul Retrieval. Have you heard of it?"

"No, I'm sorry. I haven't," I responded, as I did a quick once-over of the leaflet.

Continuing to smile, she said, "Look over the flyer and give it some thought. We're just around the corner. The address is at the bottom. Feel free to join us if you're free."

I thanked her and read the flyer. It talked about retrieving parts of our soul (the parts we give up during our lives or those parts that are taken from us unwillingly). It all sounded interesting, but I knew I had to get down to Santa Fe. I would not be going to the seminar. I'll be going to my own soul retrieval seminar in a couple of days, I thought. Maybe that was what this trip was about. There is no doubt that my soul needed some work and perhaps even some retrieval. I hoped to God that this trip would offer me learning that was deeper.

I finished breakfast, mounted the bike and pointed it south toward Santa Fe. I was just seventy miles from where my Vision Quest would begin. The ride dropped in altitude all the way and I took my time, often stopping to enjoy some gorgeous views. I was both excited and nervous, hoping I was up to the challenge. At the edge of town, I pulled into a gas station to fill-up and give Jack a call.

"Hello Will," he said in a welcoming voice. "Welcome to Santa Fe." He gave me instructions to a Buddhist retreat on the edge of town, the place where the seven participants would spend a day and night to decompress and prepare for the Quest.

I found the place quickly and checked in at the desk, amazed at the both the beauty of the place and how relaxed it made me feel. My small, simple adobe room was tastefully decorated with handmade furniture and beautiful Mexican tile floors. A private bath with deep-set windows in adobe walls revealed beautiful gardens outside. My eyes were drawn to several hummingbirds through the window. I stood mesmerized by the sight; the first time I had ever seen so many hummingbirds together. I smiled, wondering, 'Perhaps there's a meaning in this'?

I unpacked, showered, and went into the central living area, a combination of kitchen, reading area, and conversation nooks. Large timbers, adobe walls and Mexican floor tiles gave the place a comfortable southwestern charm. The space was quiet and reflective, as I would have expected for this kind of retreat.

"Feel free to make a cup of tea any time you need one," said a friendly lady who walked by. "Make the place yours while you're here," she added with a smile.

I thanked her and brewed a cup from the large selection of herbal teas. When it was ready, I walked out onto the rear veranda and took a seat in a comfortable chair with deep cushions. More of the hummingbirds made their way to nearby flowers, stealing my attention. The Retreat was situated against a National Forest, with beautiful views of the high desert and forest. It was nice to just sit and not have to think about anything. I could feel that this was a spiritual place and tried to absorb as much of it as I could.

I heard a squeak as the screen door behind me opened.

"Will? I'm Jack."

I turned to see an extended arm greeting me from a man of about fifty. Thin, fit and tanned, he looked comfortable in jeans, a natural fiber shirt and outdoor boots. I stood and shook his hand.

"Jack! Nice to meet you! I want to thank you for having me aboard for the Quest."

He answered with a smile, "You're the one who decided to be aboard, Will. It was you who knew you needed to be here. You'll understand more about that later. You had asked about a place to store your bike while out on the Quest?"

"Yes, is there somewhere I can do that?"

"That's not a problem. I'd be happy to have you leave it in my garage. I live just about a mile from here. If you'll follow me over, we'll put it inside and then I can drop you back here. I'm picking up a couple of the other participants at the airport after that. The rest of the group is driving in. The plan for tonight is to pick all of you up at 7:00 and then go to a great Mexican restaurant. Sound good?"

"Sounds great," I said, as I grabbed my keys to the bike.

I followed Jack to his place just a short mile away. It was a small home of cedar and glass, also on the edge of the Santa Fe National Forest. Furnished simply and tastefully, it was clear that he was not into accumulating things. There was no TV, but plenty of books. An avid reader myself, I felt immediately comfortable in the place. Hanging off the small upstairs outdoor deck were Buddhist prayer flags that had clearly been up for some time. I asked Jack about them and he explained,

"These prayer flags are said to bring happiness and long life to those who hang them. They're often hung on homes, inside and out. It's said they also provide beneficial vibrations for the area nearby. I leave them up until they finally come apart with age. Then I take them down and burn what remains." He looked at his watch and said, "We better get the bike inside and go. I need to pick up a couple of folks at the airport."

I wrestled the 850 lb. motorcycle down the steepest loose-gravel driveway imaginable, wondering if I could keep it from sliding out from under me. It was all I could do to avoid an embarrassing fall. Finally, I reached the bottom and rolled it inside Jack's garage. We climbed back up the steep slope to his 4x4 and drove back to the retreat. There wasn't time for a long talk, but I felt comfortable enough with this man to tell him of the unexplained fears I had been feeling on the trip.

"Respect those fears, Will. They're telling you something. That's what this Quest is about ... getting in touch with yourself at a core level, including facing your fears. The combination of connecting with nature and giving up the load you carry will give you the chance to deal with those fears."

After a few moments of silence, he said, "You might consider visiting the open market today. It's about eight blocks from the retreat. It's a place where Native Americans sell jewelry, drums and rattles. You should consider getting a drum or rattle. Try them out, and then listen to your heart while you're there. We'll talk about the use of drums and rattles at base camp tomorrow night. I'm going by the market on the way to the airport. How about I drop you off?"

I agreed and we drove the several blocks to the market. I jumped out and thanked him.

"No problem, Will. See you at 7:00. It was good to meet you!"

"Same here, Jack. See you later." I watched him drive off and then took a look around to see dozens of Native Americans laying out their jewelry, drums and rattles onto beautiful Indian blankets on the ground. There was a wide selection of drums and rattles. I held several of the smaller drums and tried them out, doing the same with the rattles. I finally settled on a small rattle. It looked like some sort of hollow natural wood tube, filled with seeds or small rocks. I stepped up to pay the elderly Native American lady.

With a smile, and no doubt sensing my lack of knowledge, she asked,

"Would you like a booklet on how to use this?"

Smiling at her, I responded,

"Yes, I would. Thank you. Was it that obvious?"

Still smiling, she said, "Most folks have not had experience with them, so you're not alone." She handed me a small booklet that explained how rattles and drums were used in ceremonial rituals. Thanking her again, I continued to shop and I found some beautiful dream catcher earrings for my wife. I paid for everything and began the eight-block walk back to the retreat.

At seven that evening, I walked out to the parking lot where the other six participants were assembling with Jack. He asked for the group to gather around for introductions. It was an interesting mixture of people, five men and two women. Frank, a thirty-five year-old jeweler from Chicago; Mike and Andrea, a just-married young couple from Albuquerque; Barbara, a fiftyish radio personality from California; Stan, a fortyish Hollywood producer; and Mike, a twenty-five year-old from Santa Fe on his second Vision Quest experience with Jack.

There was also one coach from Iowa.

Jack introduced his friend Martin, who gave us a bit of background on why the two of them led people on vision quests. Martin spoke from the heart as he told the group that both he and Jack had experienced their own very special spiritual journeys. Both had felt a calling to lead others to do the same. After the introductions, we loaded up into three vehicles and made our way to Jack's favorite Mexican restaurant. The food and the company were incredible. It was an impressive group of people ranging from nineteen to fifty-four years of age, all of us excited about the impending Quest.

Jack mentioned that we would leave early in the morning for a visit to a Native American kiva, a spiritual underground prayer room where we would share our motivations for undertaking the Quest. Back at the retreat that evening, we sat over tea, talking and further getting to know one another. I was beginning to feel more comfortable about everything. It was clear to me that there were others on the same search as me.

The following morning, we loaded ourselves into three four-wheel drive vehicles and made our way to the kiva, located several miles North of Santa Fe. We assembled above the entrance as Jack explained that a kiva was a sunken earthen prayer room and that we should descend into it only with good intentions and a commitment to deep personal reflection. He also mentioned that the Dali Lama had recently visited this special place and had blessed the space. Jack asked us to free our hearts in prayer, to be open and honest with our feelings, and when ready, to descend into the prayer room.

Martin swung open a door crafted into the ground and we climbed down a handcrafted wooden ladder into an earthen circle of about a 25' radius. After lighting candles, we sat on ledges formed into the walls, facing the center of the space. After a couple of minutes of silent reflection, Martin lit some dried sage bound into a smudge stick and came around to each of us gently waving the sage and its smoke around our heads and shoulders. I was amazed by the ritualistic nature of it all.

Jack then spoke quietly to the group,

"This is the second step of the Vision Quest experience. You have listened to your souls and chosen to be here. That was the first step. I honor you for that. I would like each of you to speak to the group, if you feel compelled, to share with us why you are here and what you hope to get out of the experience. Please be honest. Nothing will go beyond the kiva."

Jack picked up a stick lying beside his seat. About 20" long, it looked to be of a finely finished wood and had a leather wrap around each end. He explained that it was a prayer stick and that each of us would hold it while speaking. When done, we would pass it to the person on our right. Looking at me, seated to his right, he asked,

"Will, would you go first, please?"

I had no time to prepare my thoughts, so I made the choice to let my heart speak for me. I took the stick, took a deep breath, and stood up. I spoke about what I did for a living and how I was hoping to find my core self, to make more of a difference for those around me. I also spoke of my need to come to grips with some choices I had made in my life that could have been better. I told the group about meeting Great Thunder and the dream that had prompted this trip. Finally, I spoke to the fears that had been with me since the trip began, feeling comfortable that I could share it with the group. When finished, I passed the stick to Frank.

There were tears, laughter, and honesty as the participants spoke about their own paths. There was a lot of head nodding and I could see that we all shared many of the same motivations, concerns and fears. A short hour and a half later, all had finished. I sat quietly, reflecting on how each of us had our own reasons for being there, yet I also felt a shared experience unfolding between us.

Jack, holding the prayer stick again, then stood and spoke, "Each of you is here for very personal and special reasons. Martin and I are your guides to aid you through the process. You, however, will control your experience, and determine if it is successful. I believe all of you are here with the right heart. I'll leave you to a few moments of silent prayer and meditation. When you're ready, I'll meet you outside the kiva."

We sat with our own thoughts, in quiet reflection, as Jack and Martin climbed the ladder to the outside world. I prayed that I would understand the purpose and meaning of what was about to unfold and that I would understand my fears. I also prayed that the others on this Quest would find meaning in their own experiences.

After climbing out of the kiva, we assembled by the vehicles where Jack again addressed the group,

"Tomorrow will be a big day for all of you. There will be a drive of about two hours to where we'll leave the road. We'll then drive off-road for another twelve miles. We can four-wheel drive most of it, but will likely need to carry our gear the last two miles because we cross a stream that is too deep for the vehicles to get across when it rains. Once we are well into the canyons, we will look for a good place for base camp. Each of you will find a good spot for your own tent, where you can see the kitchen area that we will set up. You will spend a day at base camp, with an evening meeting around a campfire. First aid training, as well as training in Native American spirituality, will be covered. The canyons are known for both rattlesnakes and scorpions. Martin and I know how to deal with both, but remember, you will be out there alone and must know what to do if there is a problem. You will pair up for safety. This means that you and a partner will create a rock pile between your two sites, where you will go each day at different, designated times. You will add a rock to your pile each day you are out. If you don't leave a rock, it means there is a problem and your partner must then go to your site. If everything goes smoothly, there will be no actual contact with another person during the time on your Quest. Once we set up at the base camp area, you will each have several hours to go on a solo hike to look for a spot where you can do your Quest. Open your heart and listen to the cues around you to aid you in finding your site. You will leave base camp on Wednesday morning after breakfast and return to camp Sunday morning, thus you will be out five days and four nights. We will talk more about all this at base camp tomorrow night."

We made our way back to the Buddhist Retreat where we had a light dinner of salad and soups. The group was reflective and quiet as we contemplated what was ahead. It was exciting, yet I continued to feel the underlying sense of fear that had been with me since I started the trip. While I could deal with the potential for rattlesnakes and scorpions, I was more concerned about being totally alone for five days and four nights, alone with only my thoughts. Could I do it? I was used to being immersed in a fast-paced lifestyle around people. This was going to be a big change. As I lay in the bed, I thought,

"There's no turning back now." The combination of concerns and excitement kept me awake for a very long time. Finally, and without dreams, I slept.

The next morning, we assembled in the parking lot of the retreat to begin the trip to the Quest site. After loading our gear, the three all-wheel drive vehicles departed Santa Fe, heading north. After nearly two hours on a two-lane road, we exited onto a small gravel road that quickly became nearly impassable. It was now clear why we were in 4x4 vehicles as we forged ahead for another slow ten miles. The road shrunk to nothing. We were now moving into a canyon as the walls began to rise up around us. Finally, we came to a fast flowing creek, perhaps twenty feet across.

Jack got out of the lead vehicle and motioned us to join him. "This is where we park the vehicles. If we take the vehicles across and there is a hard rain while we are out, we may not be able to get back across for a week. We'll need to unload everything and carry it to our base camp area. It will likely take three trips. Base camp will be about two miles away."

Each of us loaded ourselves up with what we could comfortably carry and followed Jack and Martin. A couple of miles later, with the canyon walls now rising several hundred feet up, Jack announced,

"I think this is the area we will use for a base camp." We set our loads down, left him to set up the kitchen, and returned to the vehicles to unload the remaining gear. After three long trips, we had everything at the campsite. It was tiring work as the loads were heavy and the altitude and dry heat were getting to me. It was clear that it was going to be hot in the canyon. After the final trip, I walked over to the base camp. I could see that Jack was well versed in putting together a camp kitchen. Large plastic tarps were stretched high between trees to protect everything from both rain and a very hot sun.

Jack called us together and said,

"Each of you should find a site near here so you can set up your own base camp tent. Try to stay within ¼ mile of the kitchen. I'd like you to meet back here in an hour. You'll have the afternoon to go out on a solo hike to look for your individual Quest site. After that, all of you should be back here by 6:00 for dinner."

I found a spot within a couple hundred yards of the base camp that felt right and set up my small tent. We assembled again at the kitchen area an hour later and were told to "feel out the surroundings, to listen for messages" as we went out to search for our individual Quest sites. No one would be closer than a mile to another participant in the group. Jack instructed us to listen to our intuitive sides, with the hope that we would know when the right spot presented itself. I walked for miles as I looked for a spot. With no luck, and exhausted, I saw a very large flat rock by a stream that looked like a good spot for a rest.

I took off my backpack and jumped up on the rock to rest and pray for guidance in finding a Quest site. The more I looked around, the more I realized that this was a very nice spot. It was near a creek and had beautiful grass all around. The large, flat rock was about five feet above the canyon floor, about twenty feet across, and looked as if it had fallen from the canyon wall at some point in the past. It was perfect for sitting and meditating. I felt very relaxed and knew this would be the place where I would spend the next five days.

I was in a large canyon with a moderate number of young trees, none over twenty feet in height. The grass was surprisingly thick and green for being in a canyon at this altitude. While I was within thirty feet of the canyon wall behind me, it was at least a quarter mile across the canyon to the other wall. The rugged canyon walls were totally vertical and looked impossible to climb. They looked to be approximately 300 feet tall at their peak. A creek, perhaps five feet across, ran within fifteen feet of the large rock. It was a tranquil place, and I knew I was where I needed to be. I said a prayer of thanks for being guided to this spot.

Upon return to the base camp the group met and, for safety reasons, discussed the general locations of the spots. Our safety net would be the rock piles. As Jack again described the process of the rock piles, we paired-up based on whose sites were the closest. My partner would be Mike, the young man who had come on the Quest with his new wife. They would be separated, and I could tell his wife was scared of the process and the time alone. Jack, sensing this, offered to be her partner. Mike and I had seven gallons of water to carry to each of our sites, and we helped each other, thus insuring we would know how to get to each other if there was a problem. At a point mid-way between our sites, we each made a circle of rocks next to each other. Each day we would travel to the rock pile at different times to add a rock to the center of the circles. This would be our signal that things were OK. If all went well, there would be five rocks in each pile at the end of the Quest.

After a wonderful dinner of sandwiches made with fresh organic vegetables, cheeses and chips, we gathered around the campfire to discuss what lay ahead. Jack first spoke a bit about his background in sustainable resources and farming practices. His own spiritual quest had led him along a path that now had him mentoring and leading others down their own spiritual paths. I could tell that he was deeply committed to treating the earth with respect and making it a healthier place for an ever-increasing population to live. We then went around the circle offering a bit more about our lives and reiterating why we were on the Quest.

We were asked to speak to any fears we had in the process. I felt better, knowing that I was not the only one with concerns of what was ahead. Jack then offered to give anyone some tobacco if we wished to use it for prayer while on our Quest. I declined, having bought some loose tobacco while in Santa Fe.

A discussion about first aid techniques followed, including how we would communicate with others if we encountered a problem. Concerned about snake and scorpion bites, I had brought a snakebite kit with me. It gave me some confidence, but I had yet to open it. I made a mental note to read the instructions in the morning.

After an evening get-together around a fire, and a final meal, Martin told us that upon waking we would neither be eating nor speaking. We would maintain silence as we began our entry into the Quest. I decided to sleep outside my small tent on this final night in base camp. A star-filled night was the reward. As I surveyed the heavens, it prompted memories of those nights sleeping outside of Great Thunder's cabin. I was excited beyond words, yet I slept well.

The Vision Quest
Day 1

I awoke from a deep sleep and packed the few things I would take with me. I took off my wristwatch, left it in my tent and made my way to where the others were already assembled. There would be no breakfast on this day. The seriousness of the moment, magnified by our silence, was obvious to all. One at a time, each of us stepped into a prayer circle that Jack and Martin had laid out with rocks on the ground. While in the circle, we received quiet prayers from the others and a dusting of smoke from the smudge stick. We had been told the night before that this ritual was provided to help us give up the emotional baggage we carried into the Quest. I knew I had to leave these issues in the circle so that my experience could be more internalized at a core level. I had yet to begin the Quest, and already I felt emotionally drained. Still, I was excited beyond words that it was finally beginning.

Martin looked me in the eye, and after a few seconds, nodded as he squeezed my arm. I left the circle and began my long walk to my site. I carried only my journal, rain gear, a plastic tarp, my rattle, a snakebite kit, and my sleeping bag. I also carried the letter from Great Thunder. I would have no watch, no camera, and no phone.

The next five days would turn out to be some of the most spiritual days of my life. My concerns were many: Would I be hungry? Could I handle the demands of the experience with no food? Could I be alone that long? How would my body react to not having my daily coffee fix? I smiled as I thought: all of these are minor issues. There would be much bigger fish to fry over the next several days as I struggled with concerns about relationships, both past and present. I hoped my prayers would be heard.

As I walked the several miles to my site, I thought about all the things that had happened in the past three years that led to this day. I wondered if Great Thunder would know that I was on this Quest. I had a feeling he did. As I walked through the canyon, I felt good, thinking, I'm so glad to finally be on the Quest.

I made it to my site, climbed up on the rock, and surveyed the top of the canyon wall against the sky. It had finally begun. I walked to the nearby creek and found a number of baseball-sized rocks. Taking several, I laid out a circle near the rock with a diameter of about 8 feet. Using the path of the sun as my guide, I placed larger rocks to show East, South, West, and North. The soft grass within the circle would provide excellent ground for praying. Looking ahead, I knew I would be in that circle throughout the final night of the Quest. After placing the rocks, I pulled out some loose tobacco and sprinkled it around the circle as an offering. I prayed that the area be a special space of power, energy, and healing. I also said a prayer to the animals in the area to accept me as a non-threatening visitor. I meant no harm to any animal and only wished to share their space peacefully for five days.

I spent the afternoon scouting around the area, before returning to the rock and pulling out the letter from Great Thunder.

God is everywhere, in every rock, tree, blade of grass and animal. Respect them all and they will help guide you when they are needed.

I had been told that the canyon was alive with animal and plant life; all of which were to be my partners on this journey. I sat quietly on the rock, sponging up the radiant heat coming from it and looking closely at the surroundings. The canyon was beautiful. For such a dry area of New Mexico, I marveled at the beauty around me. The grass was a vibrant green, perhaps four to five inches tall. There were no weeds. The trees, approximately fifteen feet apart, were no taller than twenty feet and looked to be pines. We had learned, at the campfire talk of the previous evening, that there was a great deal of animal life in this canyon. Jack had recommended that we each pray, asking that the animals allow us to be there. I had done that, asking that the animal life know that I was there for personal growth only and that I would mean no harm to any animal. Jack had put it in perspective when he said, "If you show love and appreciation to the wildlife, they will not be afraid of you. They can feel when someone wants to harm them. Show respect and appreciation and you will not have an issue."

I looked around, wondering if I would see animals while on the Quest. That question was soon answered. While I sat quietly on the rock, reflecting on my mission here, a small chameleon, light green in color, climbed onto the rock. It moved toward me, stopping about five feet away. It sat quietly and stared at me for over a minute. I looked at it, not speaking, but thinking positive thoughts. Thank you for letting me be here. I'll treat my time here with respect. The chameleon stayed a while longer and finally, in no hurry, turned and sauntered off the rock.

My first encounter, I thought. I lay back to take a short nap. The sun was high and hot, but it was a dry heat, and I was not uncomfortable. I wondered how cool it might get in the evening, especially if it rained. I was concerned about having enough clothing to stay warm and dry if faced with bad weather. I did bring a rain jacket and rain pants with me. I hoped it was enough.

When I awoke, the sun had moved beyond the walls of the canyon. It was a beautiful site as soft white clouds raced quickly across a bright blue sky framed by the walls of the canyon. After watching the clouds for a while, I noticed they were getting darker. Will we be getting rain? I wondered. Jack had warned us of how quickly powerful showers could appear in the canyon. Was the lush grass an indication of regular rains in the canyon?

It wasn't long before I could hear thunder in the distance. Without a timepiece, I didn't know the time of day, but the sun had long since passed over the canyon wall. My best guess was that it was around 5:00. As the clouds continued to get darker, I knew we were likely to get wet, and soon. I laid out the plastic tarp on the rock, put the sleeping bag on top of it, opened it, and placed my backpack there as well. I put on the rain jacket and rain pants. I knew if it rained, I had to keep my clothes and sleeping bag dry, so I decided to pull the sleeping bag around my backpack and me, and then wrap the plastic tarp around me. The top of the rock was on a slight incline, thus allowing the water to drain down under the tarp. I would stay dry. It was a good plan ... and it was needed.

Within twenty minutes, the rain began. I pulled the tarp tight around me and over my head, allowing me to look out while staying dry in the process. The rain and the wind picked up. I hoped my new friends were able to get out of this. I didn't fear the weather, even though there was lightning in the area. I could hear the thunder and see its accompanying lighting as it struck above the top of the canyon walls. The strikes were close!

I figured I was down low enough that lightning would unlikely find its way down to the canyon floor. Just after that thought, a large "crack" behind me made me jump as lightning hit somewhere on the canyon wall. Maybe it could strike down here! Having no place to get out of the weather, I simply pulled the tarp tighter around me, said a prayer and decided to watch the show. An early test, I thought with a forced smile.

    The rain lasted nearly an hour without letting up. When it finally stopped, the sky quickly cleared and I surveyed my surroundings. The creek was now louder, faster, and fuller. The smell was wonderful, a combination of negative ions from the rain and the plant life in the canyon. I laid out the plastic tarp on the rock with the sleeping bag placed over it. Everything was dry and I considered sleeping on the rock for the first night. I knew there would be many other tests ahead, beginning with hunger and caffeine withdrawal. I drank some water and returned to the top of the rock, surveying the darkening sky as the sun began to set far beyond the top of the canyon wall. I thought about the evening and the potential for danger. I knew that black bear were fairly common in the canyon, as were the ever-present rattlesnakes and scorpions. Surprisingly, I wasn't worried. I climbed off the rock and entered the prayer circle, first scattering some tobacco as an offering. I prayed for both knowledge and clarity in what I was about to face. I also prayed for my safety.

    I climbed back onto the rock to read the directions in the snakebite kit ... just in case I might need it. As I sat down, I caught the contrail of a plane in the corner of my eye, so high that there was no sound as it passed slowly toward the end of the canyon. Those folks, enclosed in a thin tube of metal, were totally unaware of what was happening below them in this canyon. Aren't we all like that? We live in our own man-made worlds, separated from nature, chasing the things we think are important. I looked around in wonder at the beauty of this place, thinking, "I wish the folks in that plane could see this place right now."

My little chameleon friend returned, climbing up onto the rock to the same place as before. Again, he stood motionless as he stared at me.

"What can I do for you?" I asked out loud. "You've come back for a reason, I'm sure. You'll have to help me, my little friend," I said. "I'm new to all this. Feel free to come by anytime." I sent positive thoughts and energy toward him, hoping it would register that I was a friendly visitor. Finally, tired of my company, he scampered away. I had a feeling he would be back.

I sat contemplating my journey thus far: my meetings with Great Thunder, the powerful dreams, and now the Vision Quest. I knew that there was real meaning to all of it. I also knew that there was likely a higher power at work. Tired, I moved the tarp and sleeping bag down to the grass where I would be more comfortable. It was only seconds before I fell asleep easily and without worries.

Vision Quest
Day 2

I awoke to an odd screeching sound, high above me. As I looked up, I could see a large bird gliding in circles at the top of the canyon wall almost directly over me. I knew it was an eagle due to the size of its wingspan and its white head and tail feathers. I sat up, immediately interested in the rare site. I had seen an eagle in a natural setting only once before, when visiting the Kennedy Space Center years ago. The wingspan and the beauty of the bird had left its imprint on me ever since. I stood and stretched as I continued to watch the great bird. It made slow circles, gliding effortlessly on thermals. Was it here to visit me, I wondered? I climbed up on the rock to watch it directly above me, perhaps 500 feet high. The top of the food chain, I thought. Two other eagles joined the large bird and they spiraled in a beautifully choreographed dance, using the thermals to stay aloft. It was an amazing sight.

It was at that moment that it struck me ... these are the animals that were in my dream several years ago ... first the chameleon, and now the eagles! It was happening just as it had in my dream! I then knew that I would likely have also an encounter with a deer while here. I remembered how Great Thunder had explained the meaning of these animals: the chameleon, a sign of an intuitive awakening and sensitivity to the environment; and the eagle, a messenger from heaven and a sign of new birth and creativity. Both were about finding a higher sense of purpose and spirituality. As I watched my new eagle friends, I gave thanks for their visit and further contemplated the meaning of their appearance.

When the sun was at its highest point in the sky, I hiked the two miles to the rock pile that Mike and I would share. I could see that he had been there as there was a small rock in his circle. I placed one in my circle and offered a quick prayer for his safety as I sprinkled a bit of tobacco around his circle.

I spent the day hiking around my camp area, immersing myself into the natural setting and being attuned to everything that I saw. How often we miss the things that matter because we focus on things that don't. I made a pledge to fully engage myself in the natural surroundings while on the Quest. Upon returning to the rock, I again pulled out Great Thunder's letter to me.

> *Listen to your intuition. We all have spirit helpers, Guardian Angels that aid us in the challenges of our lives.*
> *Yours are looking after you, but you must listen to your intuitive side.*

I do believe we all have guardian angels to help guide us through life. I also believe they speak to us through our innate intuitive powers. My grandmother once told me a powerful and personal story about intuition. When my dad was fifteen, they lived in the small town of Harrodsburg, KY, thirty miles from Lexington. One night, he had asked her to let him go to Lexington with some of his school friends. One of them, a sixteen year-old, would be driving. She had a bad feeling about it and told him he couldn't go. To say he was unhappy was an understatement. There was a confrontation, but Granny stuck to her guns. He didn't go. Later that night, that car, with four young boys in it, had a horrible crash on the way to Lexington. Some of those boys died that night. When she first told me this story, she simply said, "Sometimes you just know the right thing to do. We don't always know why we know, we just know." Her intuition had spoken to her that night, and I'm here today because she had listened.

Intuition is something I use in coaching. While coaching runners is science-based, I know enough to be flexible with workouts on days when something goes wrong, when it is clear that we will not accomplish the workout objective. The coach who listens to intuition at these moments knows to make changes. An athlete must balance many variables: training load, recovery, nutrition, rest, academics, social life, work and home life. When one of them is off, it affects the others. Intuitive coaching is, in part, the art of coaching, of seeing the big picture. It's about balancing the many variables that influence performance. At Grinnell, the academic load can be difficult, especially at exam times. An adjustment in training and racing at these times can help to maintain balance. It took time (and more than a few failures) for me to learn this. Such is the difference between knowledge and wisdom. There are many smart coaches out there who know the science of sport, but not so many who see the big picture. I have learned that knowledge is about the science of coaching, while wisdom is about the art of coaching. Both take time to develop.

I drank more water as I sat on the rock contemplating my choice of profession. Did I choose coaching, or did it choose me? While I had no intention of pursuing a coaching career while I was in college, I did want to teach in the classroom. Of course, I have learned over time that sports provide their own unique and challenging classroom. The athletic classroom for my athletes had also become a learning tool for me. I knew that this trip was telling me that I still had much to learn, especially about myself. I just hoped I could make sense of it all.

Having no camera, I spent the afternoon with pencil and journal trying to draw the canyon view from my rock. While it was clear I was no artist, I stubbornly kept at it. I wanted a memory of this special place. I was glad to be here. After a short nap, I awoke to a noise in the nearby brush. I kept still and quietly looked up to see a young doe only twenty feet away. It looked right into my eyes as I sat up, my heart racing. I had now had all three encounters that I had experienced in my dream at Great Thunder's cabin. All three! Without moving, I stared back, sending positive thoughts to it to not be scared. I wanted it to know I meant no harm. The young deer slowly ambled toward the rock, stopping only fifteen feet away. I was amazed that this was happening. Just like the dream! It was clear the young animal had no fear of me. I wished I had something to give it, but of course I had no food of any kind. I could only send it positive thoughts, which I did. I continued to look at it as it stared back at me. Finally, after several minutes, it slowly turned and walked away, probably bored with the encounter. I was in awe that the young doe had come so close without fear. Jack had said to communicate to the animals that I was here with good intentions, and I had. I remembered that Great Thunder had told me that a deer signified new perceptions and opportunities for new growth. All three animals I had encountered had to do with new direction, self-growth, and creativity. It was becoming increasingly clear what this Quest was about.

Later, I returned to the prayer circle, offering thanks for the day and my encounters with the eagles and the doe. Any fears I brought into the Vision Quest were now gone. I was both comfortable and happy to be here. I drank more water in attempt to fill my stomach with something. It seemed to be working; I did not feel hunger! More surprisingly, I was having no headaches from a lack of caffeine.

I again pulled out the letter from Great Thunder.

Live with quality, honesty and integrity in your work and life. It makes a difference to those you teach.

What is integrity? Is it doing the right things for the right reasons? I remember asking my cross-country team captains that very question a couple of years back before the fall season began. It was a special group of individuals, each having been elected captain by their peers. I had taken the three of them out to dinner at what they called a "tablecloth restaurant." I had paid for the expensive meal, but I was going to make them work for it. The goal of the dinner was to develop a team covenant. Many coaches have used team contracts to define the "rules" of participation in their programs, something with which I have always had a fundamental issue with. A contract is based on distrust between two parties. One party simply does not trust the other, so they each sign a document as a promise to follow through with an agreement. I know that for a team to function at the highest level there has to be something much stronger than a contract behind it. The participants need to commit to each other at a level far deeper than what a piece of paper can provide. After several hours of discussion and using some concepts of a gifted and respected coaching colleague, Joe Vigil, the team captains and I came up with the following document:

THE TEAM COVENANT
Purpose

The purpose of the Grinnell Cross Country Program is to help each runner improve as a runner. It is also about giving people opportunities for growth that will prepare them for post-running life. Creating fast runners is important. Creating stronger people is more important.

Self-Governance

You are responsible for your team. That is, you work at a variety of levels to build, maintain, and contribute to the development of the team. You are accountable for your choices. Take ownership for your actions, opinions, and beliefs. You are accountable for preventing your actions from infringing or violating others' rights. You are responsible for speaking and listening to others to reach shared understandings. You are responsible for addressing situations and communicating concerns about issues that undermine community or individual rights.

The Goals of Grinnell Cross Country
- *To see every runner improve*
- *To be successful as a team at conference and national levels*
- *To help the runner develop healthy values*
- *To provide an outlet from academics at Grinnell*
- *To make new friends and to manage relationships*
- *To foster a healthy lifestyle*
- *To create a supportive team culture*

Accountability
The rules for Grinnell Cross Country are few... but they are important.
- *Be on time for training and departure for meets.*
- *Follow the training plan.*
- *Know the difference between hard and easy days.*
- *Understand why we train like we do. Become a student of the sport.*
- *Respect your body and make the right choices to do so.*
- *Be an example of honor and integrity to your teammates, your school and your family.*

The Whole Runner and Full Engagement
Success in running is due to many variables working together toward an end result. Nutrition, functional training and restoration,

and healthy lifestyle choices will all influence performance. Positive health habits and choices are what create the whole runner. Becoming a student of distance running gives the runner the knowledge to succeed. Spiritual development also adds to one's wholeness. Working to become a whole person will help you be a whole runner. Being fully engaged in the process is a must. As Dr. Joe Vigil says, "Success comes from a burning passion to succeed...success does not come from an obsession." Know the difference.

Mental Toughness

This sport is one of pain. Learning to deal with pain is a part of the training process. Learning to be mentally tough and (to have courage) is a learned phenomenon. Training is what teaches this. Challenge yourself to face challenge and pain in your training...that is where courage is learned.

Relationships and Support

Nothing is more important to a team than relationships. Every team has the potential for greatness, but each runner must find his role, be fully engaged and offer what he can give to the team. When interpersonal problems develop, deal with them immediately, whether between athletes or between coach and athlete.

Consistency, Discipline and Quality

Consistency in training is what results in optimal performance over time. Develop habits that result in consistent training. Discipline is an internal choice to be consistent and focused. Champions are consistent and focused in their training. The quality of work will dictate the level of success. Do all things well, no matter how small. This is how you build self-confidence and self-belief.

Honor and Integrity

Respecting yourself and your teammates, and the work that you do, is what honor is about. It is also about doing what is right. Most of all, honor is about standing with, and by, your teammates. To run faster is a goal of the program. To do this with teammates, and with honor and integrity, is a greater goal. Your own moral and ethical code will determine your actions in life. Honor your teammates, your school, your parents, the sport, and most of all, yourself. Remember that character is not who we are, but what we do.

In writing that document, we defined why runners run and the things that matter in that process, especially what it means to be part of a team. It was an exercise in defining both quality and integrity. I knew that if the athletes could commit to this document on an internal level, their experience in the program could be something far greater than they imagined it could. It really was about more than running. I could not have been more proud of my captains. They were able to put onto the paper the things that really mattered in the sport experience. This covenant was a true reflection of an athlete-centered model of coaching. It explained our previous successes and also provided a blueprint for future successes in the program.

I laid back on the big rock, looked up to the darkening blue sky and thought about the life cycle we all go through. We're born as pure, innocent souls. Then life quickly starts to shape us from the outside. That pure soul is tested through the experiences of social learning. We begin to feel the need to please others or to be better than others, sometimes both. As we get older and wiser, we begin to realize the limitations of being driven by external motivations. Hopefully that recognition inspires us to search for our inner selves. That process is not always a smooth one as our inner selves have often been covered up with layers and layers of life experiences. Such is the challenge we all face as we go through the life cycle.

There are so many smart, knowledgeable people out there who have not figured it out. We continue chasing fame, fortune and happiness in ways that actually deny inner growth. An interesting thing, this life cycle. It takes wisdom, I think, to make us aware of the meaning of our paths. Of course, sometimes we have to trip over ourselves to learn what matters. That had certainly happened to me.

I finally closed my eyes. It was another good sleep.

Vision Quest
Day 3

I awoke from a deep sleep and walked to the creek to wash myself. While there, I was shocked to see black bear tracks in the mud bank ... just twenty-five feet from my sleeping bag! I hadn't heard a thing during the night. Of course, there was no reason to be scared of animals searching for food. I had none. Great Thunder had said that encountering a bear means we are coming out of hibernation; another sign of re-birth. No surprise,
I thought with a smile. Every animal I had encountered represented the same themes of rebirth and renewal. I knew why I was here. Great Thunder had told me that we shape our spirit, molding ourselves daily with the choices we make. When we choose to act with a lack of honesty or without integrity, we pay for it, both now and in the afterlife. It made

sense to me. This Native American belief was also shared by many religions.

As I climbed onto the rock, I wondered if this experience would make me a better coach. My teams had been successful in the past, but I wanted their experience to be about more than just running. Would the experience help them face what comes after running? I knew that the athlete, not the coach, had to be the prime mover in the process if real growth was to occur.

Screeching from above led me to look up. My three eagle friends were again circling above me. I smiled and watched them for a while before shifting my focus to the unique natural setting I had chosen for the Quest. The purple hue of the canyon walls shifted to golden at the top as the sunlight played off the walls. The grass and trees were alive with their bright green color. Maybe it was the rain, but this green seemed brighter than the colors I had seen when I first arrived at the site. Maybe I was just more sensitive to the beauty around me ... or maybe a lack of food was beginning to get to me.

The creek, just feet away, sang with a symphony of sound. Too often, I thought, we miss the beauty of nature. Lost in our man-made lives, we just don't take the time to really see, smell and hear what is around us. The more I looked around, the more I knew that there was nothing that man could build that could touch the beauty of nature. I watched the eagles as they continued their aerial ballet. As I sent them a silent thank you, I closed my eyes and laid back on the rock, arms spread wide to take in the energy of the place.

After a few minutes of meditation, I decided to go for a longer hike to see what was farther down the endless canyon. I put one of the water jugs in my backpack and began my trek. After hiking for twenty minutes along the canyon wall, I found a narrow walking path that appeared to climb slowly up the canyon wall. I decided to follow it to see if the climb could take me to the top. Thankful that I had hiking boots on, the path at times appeared to disappear altogether, only to reappear a few feet ahead. No wider than two feet at its widest, I became increasingly nervous at the sheer drop-off to my right. One wrong step and I knew the consequences. It took two slow hours, but I made it to the top of the canyon wall and sat to admire the view. I could feel the spiritual essence of the place as I surveyed what was beyond the canyon itself. The land at the top was devoid of trees and other vegetation. It was clear that this was the rocky, high desert of the Southwest. In comparison, the canyon below was an oasis of greenery and life. I marveled at the difference that several hundred feet of elevation, and some water, could make. After a short rest, and aided by gravity and newly found confidence, I made a much quicker trek back down to the canyon bottom. As I returned to my site, I felt amazed that the difficult climb had not been as physically taxing as I had expected. I had been without food for three days, yet I felt great.

That evening, I sat in the prayer circle and gave more thanks for the natural setting around me and for the animal encounters. Feeling more comfortable with each day, I knew I was allowing myself to fully engage with the place. I was neither hungry nor suffering from caffeine withdrawal. Much more significantly, I no longer felt the fears I had brought with me.

I thought about how my long spiritual search had begun in earnest by an event that occurred 12 years earlier. While on an earlier sabbatical leave from my college in 1988, my wife and I were in Canada working with athletes at the government-funded High Performance Training Center in Toronto. The birth of my son Cameron two years earlier had made me think hard and often about the things that really mattered in life. I was feeling a strong urge to write while on the sabbatical leave, yet wasn't sure how to put onto paper the things I was feeling. I was stuck with writer's block for several weeks, until one day, while on the way to the training facility, a short story formed in my mind. I still get chills thinking about the clarity and power of how the story took shape.

We were making our daily trip from Hamilton to Toronto in our VW camper bus when the story came to me out of the blue. I asked my wife to grab a pad of paper and I outlined the story to her as I drove, with it coming into my head faster than I could tell it. Later that evening, I took out a small micro-recorder and went for a long walk alone. Following the outline, I told the story into the tape recorder. The short fable that resulted, a children's story for adults, was published as it came off the tape, not a single word being changed. To this day I still revel in how that could have happened. It was just a little story about a young kangaroo...

> *In the central lowlands of Australia, there lived a troop of special kangaroos. The greatest jumpers in all of continent, they were respected by all of the animal kingdom for their great athletic ability. This is the story of a very special lesson learned by one of them.*

The sun had begun its ascent over the Great Dividing Range, filtering its warmth over channel country. It was here that Australia's best jumper called home. Christian, the second of five athletic kangaroos in his family, had developed into the finest jumper of them all. As the champion of all of Queensland, he was busy preparing for the opportunity to meet the best jumpers in all of Australia. It was his chance to prove that he was the best.

On this special day, his closest kangaroo friend, Cameron, abruptly awakened Christian from his sleep.

"Christian, wake up! The True Leader wishes to see you!"

Christian slowly stirred, asking,

"Wha-what? Wh-why me? Whatever for?"

"I don't know, Christian," his friend replied, "but he's waiting for you across the prairie as we speak."

Christian arose and made his way across the grassy camp area and into the prairie, all the time wondering why he had been summoned to see the True Leader. None of the kangaroos knew when the True Leader had become the head kangaroo, only that it had happened a very long time ago. Nor did they know how it had happened, only that it had.

The True Leader smiled as Christian approached.

"Good morning, Christian, my fine lad," he said with a deep resonance. "Congratulations on your fine jumping of this season. I expect your success in becoming the best jumper in all of Queensland had made you very proud."

"Thank you, True Leader," replied Christian respectfully, "I did my very best for our pack."

"And I would have expected no less from you, young Christian," the wise one said.

The young kangaroo then asked, somewhat apprehensively,

"True Leader, why have I been summoned to see you? Have I done something wrong?"

"No, not at all," he replied with a hearty laugh. "I've called you for a very special reason, a reason that should not scare you. It will become clear as our time together passes."

The answer did little to ease Christian's concern.

"I, I don't understand," he stammered.

Reading the concern on young Christian's face, the wise one said,

"Don't try to answer all questions at once, young Christian. The way to understanding is never over the short course."

After a moment to let Christian absorb the statement, he continued,

"You must have been very proud to stand on the highest platform following the competition. Wasn't it the longest jump ever for a Queensland kangaroo?"

Christian responded with a smile,

"Yes, True Leader. And yes, I was very proud. I trained for many months to be the champion. I suppose I would've been very disappointed if I hadn't won."

Christian was bursting with pride as he realized that he had earned an audience with the True Leader due to his jumping success. The wise one had wanted to bestow accolades on him for his triumph. He couldn't wait to share the news with his friends and fellow jumpers, something sure to increase his stature within the community.

The True Leader interrupted his thoughts.

"I'd like you to think about something, my young Christian," he said as he gazed into the eyes of the young kangaroo. "Please think this over carefully. What is it that you have learned from this triumph of yours in becoming the greatest jumper in all of Queensland? You were wonderful," he added, "but what have you learned from the experience? Think about this and we'll continue our talk tomorrow."

Christian began his hop across the prairie and back to camp. The True Leader watched him grow smaller against the horizon, seeing a talent in the young kangaroo of which Christian knew not.

As he went through the day, Christian was perplexed by the question posed by the True Leader. "What have I learned?" he asked himself many times, unaware of the answer. The various activities of the day became secondary as he found himself lost in his thoughts.

"Why is the True Leader so different than the rest of us? Isn't he just another kangaroo like me?" Yet Christian knew that there was something special about the old one. "It's like he functions on a different level than the rest of us. He seems so peaceful and calm." Christian then reasoned that it was the many years of experience that made for the difference, and he continued his daily routine of duties.

Later that afternoon, a group of young wallabies visited the camp with the hope of seeing the new Queensland jumping champion. Not one to disappoint them, Christian pushed himself through an exhausting workout, urged on by the spirited support of the youngsters. Christian was highly motivated by the looks of hero worship on their faces, ending the workout only because the setting sun would allow for no more.

That evening, Christian slept fitfully as he grappled with the True Leader's question. As his eyes surveyed the star-filled sky, he thought to himself,

"The True Leader lives with us, and loves us, yet rarely calls one of us to see him. So, why me? Does this gift of mine have something to do with our meeting? OF COURSE! THAT'S IT! It's this gift of mine, my ability to jump, that I can share with others! I felt a special feeling today when jumping for the young wallabies." Finally, the young kangaroo slept, confident that he had found the answer to the True Leader's question.

The next morning, Christian again approached the True Leader, sure that the wise one would be proud of his reflections during the night.

"True Leader, I believe I have the answer to your question."

"Wonderful, my son," the old one replied, with a caring smile. "Please sit and elaborate."

Christian sank to the soft grass and began.

"Obviously, True Leader, I have a very special gift to offer. If I were not to test my ability to jump, I couldn't face the less fortunate kangaroos who don't have such a gift. This must be my challenge in life--to see how far I can jump, to be the best." Christian then elaborated on how the young wallabies had come to camp to see him jump in practice, and how they had shown such great respect for him.

"Isn't this what you wanted to hear, True Leader?" Christian asked upon finishing.

The wise one looked far off over the plain, his mind many miles away. Finally, he spoke.

"My young Christian, let me tell you a story. Many years ago, long before you were born, I, like yourself, was a jumper. I trained many years to be the best jumper in Australia, a goal that I eventually achieved."

"True Leader!" exclaimed Christian, astonished at what he had just heard. "I... we... I had no idea that you were a jumper and that you had achieved such success. Why does no one know this?" With a loving smile, the Leader said,

"You shall see why. But first let me continue with my story." Christian sat spellbound as the True Leader went on. "It was near the Tanami Desert that I traveled to compete against the best jumpers in all of Australia. After winning, I couldn't wait to share my triumph with my friends. I'd followed my training model just as my coach had dictated, and I'd won, just as he knew I would." Then he paused, "Yet, I wasn't happy."

"But True Leader," Christian responded with concern, "How could you not be happy? Weren't you the best in all of Australia?"

"You will learn why, young Christian. I want you to meet me tonight when the moon is high and the other kangaroos are asleep. Meet me on the western plain near Lake Philippi. Don't share any of our conversation with the others. They aren't ready."

Christian returned to camp with many questions on his mind. He spent the remainder of the day with his chores and jump training, yet his mind was far away. He was excited by the prospect of understanding the meaning of his meeting with the True Leader.

Later, as the moon rose high in the sky, and the other kangaroos were asleep, Christian quietly arose and made his way to the western plain near Lake Philippi, as he had been instructed. It was easy to spot the imposing figure of the True Leader as he approached.

"I'm here, True Leader." Christian said.

"This I see, Christian. Thank you for coming. I'd like to continue my story of this morning," he said as they sat on the soft grass, wet with the dew of the evening. "After becoming the champion of Australia, I retired from competing, and soon thereafter was appointed the head jumping coach of the pack from which I had come. I was very motivated to coach, yet I quickly became disillusioned. It seemed that every young jumper had all the answers, and no one cared to listen to me for advice. So, I acquired a whistle in order to whip them into shape. It was beautiful watching the team develop. They followed my orders and quickly became a 'group of one.' Yet...they seemed unhappy. As well, the quality of their jumping began to decline. Why do you think this might have happened, Christian?"

"Perhaps, True Leader, they were spoiled and didn't have the value of hard work and discipline that you had."

"Ah, my son, that's just what I thought. So I began to work them even harder. I had them eat together, train together, even live together, separate from the other kangaroos. I wanted to create the finest set of jumpers that Australia had ever known, and I believed that I knew what kind of kangaroo they needed to be for success to occur."

"And did it work, True Leader?" Christian asked.

"No, Christian, it didn't. The harder I pushed them to be model athletes, the worse they performed."

"Is that why you no longer coach, True Leader?" asked Christian.

"But Christian, I still coach, just in a more effective manner," he replied with a knowing smile. He continued, "Let me show you something. Please walk off the current best jump of all time... the world record hop." Christian paced the distance as asked, wondering what was to come.

"Now watch, Christian, said the leader. The old one took several short hops toward Christian and took off with a power and grace that Christian had never before seen. The True Leader landed just beyond the point that Christian had marked in the grass, touching down as light as a feather.

Christian, stunned by what he had seen, stammered,

"True Leader! How... how did you do that? That was the longest jump in history! How could you do that?"

The True Leader smiled and motioned Christian to have a seat. They again sat on the damp grass as the True Leader began to speak.

"How did I do it? The answer is quite simple, really. I believed myself into that jump. I believed that I was capable of that jump and simply let nothing block me from doing it. And that, my young Christian, is where real success lies. I wasn't trying to prove myself to you or anyone else, or trying to better another kangaroo. Would it make me happier to show this power to others?

"No!" he answered himself. "Authentic success is found within. Believing and accepting ourselves for who we are is the big first step toward happiness."

A tear rolled down Christian's furry cheek as he contemplated what he had learned.

"I see now, True Leader," he said softly. "I've been chasing the opportunity to prove to others that I'm a success. I've been so caught up with proving something to others that I haven't been able to see that I'm the one who must first believe in me."

"My son..." the True Leader softly replied with a nod, "you are learning." And then he smiled, adding, "Your jumping ability... isn't it just one of many tools that you can use to challenge yourself? And would it not be an insult to the Creator for us to think that we are only here on this earth to prove something to others? It doesn't matter what others think of you, only what you think of you."

The True Leader remained quiet for several moments to allow Christian to absorb his wonderful discovery.

Finally, Christian spoke,

"*True Leader, there must be many unhappy animals in this world who have not learned to accept themselves, who feel that they must constantly prove themselves, even if at the expense of others.*"

"*Yes, my son, how right you are. Isn't this the greatest challenge of life... to learn to love and accept ourselves before we can do the same for others?*"

After a few moments to contemplate his discovery Christian said,

"*True Leader, am I capable of such a jump as you have shown tonight?*"

"*Without a doubt, my son*" he replied. "*Think about what you have learned tonight. You have many gifts to offer this world, just as we all do. Think about how you can use them.*"

With that, the wise one hopped off across the plain, leaving Christian alone in the moonlight. For the first time in his short life, he felt fully alive as he contemplated the future.

Christian then hopped to the mark he had placed for the True Leader. "*I do believe in me,*" he said over and over. Then, he crouched and took off with a lightness and confidence he had never before experienced. Soaring well past the landing point of the True Leader, he finally touched down.

"*I DID IT! I DID IT!*" Christian had never known or felt such happiness, nor had he felt such peace with himself. "*I do believe in me!*" he told himself. "*I can do anything!*" Tears of happiness rolled down his cheeks, as he now understood why the True Leader led the pack as he did. The True Leader was allowing the kangaroos to find their own answers, their own truths, and to find themselves. It was not something that another could do for you. "*My big challenge in life,*" Christian thought, "*is in learning to love and accept myself before being able to help others.*"

After that special evening, and with little else to prove, Christian only jumped for the enjoyment of the sport. The True Leader eventually died and moved on to another world and new challenges. Christian became the new leader. While many champion jumpers came from his troop, even more happy and confident kangaroos also did. His kangaroos never tired of challenging themselves, and they never stopped growing. And Christian never forgot the lesson he'd learned.

Many years have passed since I wrote the fable of Christian Kangaroo. I wish I could say that brief moment of inspiration had changed the way I lived my life. After all, the way it came to me made it clear that the message was important. I'm afraid the truth is that very little changed. What had come to me in a brief moment of spiritual recognition was an opportunity lost. I knew I had been living a fortunate life, but something was missing and I knew it. I had a lot to learn about the things that really mattered. My writing about a special Kangaroo did initiate many years of reading, with the hope of finding deeper meaning to my life. I grew in knowledge, but not necessarily in wisdom or spirit. I read many books, wrote many stories, and experienced many different religions. I knew I had plenty to learn about me before I could put it all together and define my own path. The Vision Quest had allowed me to focus on working on myself. I challenged myself to use the next day and night to get to the core of who I was. I just hoped I had the courage to go there.

It had been a very good day and sleep again came easily at the end of it.

Vision Quest
Day 4

I awoke thirsty. I had roped my plastic jugs of water together and placed them in the creek to keep cold. I grabbed one and drank deeply. Again, I felt no hunger. It had now been days since I had eaten. I washed up at the creek before returning to the rock to continue my attempt to draw the site in my journal. As I drew, the eagles reappeared, offering support as they floated silently above me on the thermals.

Finally, frustrated with my lack of artistic ability, I gave up on the drawing, and shifted instead to writing in the journal. Today would be a day of focusing on relationships. As I wrote, my thoughts drifted to the many wonderful people I had been fortunate to meet in my life, especially those who had acted as mentors and guides to me. I also thought about those whom I had hurt in my life, feeling both a sense of guilt and a need to pray for forgiveness. In our shared talks in the kiva, Jack had been made it clear that, if our hearts were pure, we had the potential to make spiritual connections with those who have touched our lives. I spent a long day in the circle, both praying for forgiveness and giving thanks to those who had touched my life. I hoped they would feel my positive thoughts.

The solitude of the Quest experience was allowing me to access my soul in a way that everyday life could not. I had left all burdens in the rock circle as I walked away from base camp, so my mind was free to focus on past relationships that had been buried by years of living. It was a gratifying experience, as I felt free to finally deal with things that had pained me over the years: mistakes I had made, relationships gone bad, and things I had done that I wished I could call back. It was a long day of reflection and prayer.

The chameleon, perhaps becoming more comfortable with me, visited twice on day four and was staying for increasingly longer periods. I did my best to open my mind and heart to it, as I tried to figure out what its message was. I was just content to have company.

This would be the final night of my Quest. I would try to stay awake all night as I prayed to God for direction and meaning in my life. I readied my backpack for the sunrise hike back to base camp in the morning and laid my sleeping bag out in the circle to sit on. I knew this night would be the biggest challenge of the Quest.

That final evening defined solitude for me. I spread most of the remaining tobacco around the prayer circle and prayed for spiritual guidance for what was ahead. I had not eaten in four days, yet I felt strong and clear-headed. Maybe it's a good thing to rid our bodies of toxins and bad energy with a fast every so often. I knew I would do more fasting down the road.

As darkness fell, I began praying, shaking the rattle in a continuous, slow cadence. I thought of my parents, my grandparents and my siblings. I offered thanks for their lives and prayed for a blessing for each of them. Next, it was my wife and kids. It was hard to not tear up as I thought of all they had meant to me. I prayed that they would hear my prayers and feel the positive energy I was sending to each. Most of all, I hoped this experience would bring me home a better husband and father. I spent a great deal of time thinking of my wife that night and healing old wounds between us.

I then thought of all those who had mentored me over the years. Mentors are trusted and caring people who teach, advise and lead. The word comes from a character in Homer's epic poem *The Odyssey*. When Odysseus went to fight in the Trojan War, he entrusted the care of his kingdom to Mentor, who served as the teacher and overseer of his son, Telemachus. Perhaps more fortunate than Odysseus's son, I have been blessed to benefit from a number of mentors in my life. Relatives, neighbors, teachers and coaches -- many have had significant impact on my life.

My next-door neighbor, Dick Burton, had been my scoutmaster all the way through Explorer scouts. He was, however, far more than a scoutmaster to me. He was there for me like a father when my dad could not be. He taught me what unconditional support was.

I gave thanks for my parents. My dad decided to go to college when he was thirty-three, all while working two jobs. He earned both a Bachelor's and a Master's degree in just three and a half years. He taught me tenacity and discipline. Mom taught me about giving to others. She gave everything to us, and never asked for a thing in return.

I was fortunate to have learned from some great coaches. My high school track coach, Harold Barnett, showed unconditional support and patience as my athletic ability caught up with my passion for the sport. Jimmy Carnes, the visionary head coach at the University of Florida, and the founder of the Florida Track Club, showed me how to be a success. My pole vault coach at Florida, Walter Welsch, truly cared about me as a person first, and as an athlete second. I both cried and laughed the day I heard he had passed as I relived many fond memories of our time together on the track in Gainesville. And there was Andy Higgins, the Olympic track coach for Canada and the best man at my wedding. Andy taught me about the big picture, about balance in the sport experience. He has long been an unconditional and trusted friend.

I also thanked other coaches who had influenced me professionally through their work: Arthur Lydiard, Joe Vigil, Joe Newton, Jack Daniels, and Dan Pfaff, all internationally renowned. Vigil and Pfaff, especially, had become good friends as well as trusted professional mentors.

I thought of my coaching colleagues at Grinnell, especially the former athletic director John Pfitsch. All had impacted me in ways they would never fully know. I thanked each with a prayer and sent positive thoughts to each.

My training partners during my vaulting years, Mike Cotton and Dave Roberts, were models of friendship and support.

I also prayed hard for all those who I had hurt over the years. I was by no means a perfect angel growing up. I'd left a few girlfriends in my wake, with some relationships ending on less than perfect terms. I've long believed that when we hurt someone, we steal energy from the other party, perhaps taking a part of his or her soul in the process. Of course, with maturity, I've learned that there is an easier path to get energy from another ... and that is to first give positive energy to that person. I had certainly taken my share of energy from others, including from those I had loved. I asked forgiveness for it, hoping that I would be free of any guilt I still harbored. I prayed for God to restore the energy to each of the souls from whose energy I had taken. I also offered forgiveness to others who had harmed me over the years. I felt it was time to give up some old grudges I had stubbornly held onto. I knew the act of holding grudges would not only limit a relationship from growing, but also limit my growth. It was another example of the gap between understanding and application in my life. Yes, I still had plenty of work to do on me.

I both sat and knelt through the night as I gave thanks for the Quest experience and for the chance to connect with the natural world and God. I prayed hard, asking, "Show me what my future holds."

My arms burned from fatigue as I shook the rattle, shifting it from one hand to the other. I had no watch so I wasn't sure how long I prayed, but it was many hours. After four days and nights with no food, I was physically, spiritually, and emotionally in a very different place than I was used to. The act of fasting does strange things to your body and your mind, most of it good. It had cleared the screen of things that didn't matter, allowing me to focus on the things that did. I was very tired, but it was a good tired. Finally, with nothing left to give, I fell asleep on the grass inside the rock circle with rattle in hand.

The Dream

The dream I had that night was the most interesting and powerful of my life, so clear and intense that I wonder if it was a dream at all. In the dream, I was praying in my prayer circle at my Quest site when I looked up to see a tall, stoic Native American standing outside the circle, looking down at me. In native dress and with a long ponytail, his worn face reflected a hard life of experiences. For reasons I could not understand, I felt I could trust him. He looked at me and said, in a calm tone,

"Coach, we're going on a trip. Follow me. Do not worry. You won't be harmed."

Not really sure why, I said, "OK."

He reached out and touched my arm. With his touch, and without warning, we were suddenly going down into the earth ... and quickly! We were moving down through the soil without impediment. Amazed at what was happening, I felt no fear. Finally, we burst out into a bright, beautiful sky. I suddenly found myself sitting on the ground in a lush valley of green grass and wildflowers. What was in front of me nearly took my breath away. I had never seen so many beautiful flowers. Incredibly bright, and with great contrast, there were multiple hues of crimsons, yellows and blues. The power of the colors was almost overwhelming. The grass around the flowers was the brightest green I had ever seen. Then it struck me: there were no shadows in this place. There was a bright royal blue sky, but no sun or clouds that I could see. What added to the intensity was that I could feel the colors in some strange, unexplainable way. I could also feel some sort of connection to the trees, the grass, and even the flowers. Everything here shared a sense of harmony. I was connecting, in some strange way, with the plant life. It was an intense moment of truth, as I understood the connection between all living things.

As I observed everything in awe, the Native American said quietly,

"Now you begin to understand the bigger picture."

"Yes," I said, "Everything is connected. Not just all people, but all of life."

"Yes," he replied with a nod and an ever-so-slight smile of someone who already knew.

I jumped back as a large eagle landed directly in front of me. The chameleon and doe from my Vision Quest also appeared from behind some trees and walked up to me. They told to me that I was in the process of a rebirth. They didn't actually speak to me, but I knew what they were thinking. We could read each other's thoughts! They told me to close my eyes, which I did. I was then told to continue to make peace, through prayer, with those whom I had harmed, or had harmed me, in the past.

As soon as I processed the meaning of that thought, experiences from my past, both positive and negative, began to play themselves out in my mind. I was astonished to see events and people I had long since forgotten. As I relived my past, I could see that each of these experiences was about a relationship. In each case, I felt the emotions, not from my perspective, but from the other person's. One event played itself out after another. It was painful to see some of those moments from an earlier part of my life when I was not ready to think of others. I prayed, asking for forgiveness to those I had hurt, and was glad when it finally stopped. I was emotionally exhausted by the impact of what I had seen and felt.

I knew that both my Indian guide and the animals recognized what I was feeling. I could feel their compassion. No words were necessary. The eagle sent a message to me, "Do not be concerned about pleasing others. Such motivations do not come from within you, but from the outside. You must live your life from the inside out. You must find a way to use competition to the betterment of your athletes. It will not be easy."

My Indian guide spoke,

"Do not fear being yourself. Every living thing is a unique and special creation. When we deny our unique essence, we create both tension and pain for ourselves."

I knew he spoke the truth. After a few moments of silence and positive thoughts sent my way, the eagle nodded to me and flew off and the chameleon scampered back into the grass. The doe was the last to leave as it slowly ambled into the trees.

As I looked at my escort, I knew he could tell what I was feeling and thinking. After a few moments, he spoke,

"We learn from all experiences, good and bad. Sometimes, unfinished business makes our lives unsettled and without harmony. You are here to heal old wounds, both yours and others, and then to use what you have learned to teach others. Your coaching provides a template for you to teach things that matter. Use it well. Great Thunder gave you wise words. Read them often. There is truth in those words."

"You know Great Thunder?" I asked in awe.

He nodded, responding in a knowing way,

"Everything, and everyone, is connected. Always remember this."

I thanked him and also gave silent thanks to all living things in that beautiful place.

"We must go now," my guide said. He reached out and again touched my arm. No sooner had he made contact than we were flying back up through the earth, through cracks in the rocks, through water, through dirt, all without impediment. I had no fear. The next thing I knew, I was back in my prayer circle, alone and exhausted.

I awoke with a start, my heart hammering against my chest.

"My God!" was all I could think to say. I tried to remember it all, reliving the intensity of the images. After a while, fatigue left me too tired to stay awake, and I drifted back to sleep.

RETURN

I woke to the chirping of birds. I guessed it was between 5:00 and 6:00, still long before the sun would make its way over the canyon wall. As my mind cleared, I began to remember the dream. I quickly grabbed my journal and began writing about the experience. I was shaking as my thoughts were coming faster than I could write them down,

All of this is connected. All of us, all animal life, all plant life, even the inanimate objects around us. The goal is to find harmony.

But was harmony even possible? Mankind had managed to wreck virtually everything we had touched in the world. Maybe our only hope was through education and the development of a spirituality that could include, but also go beyond, the confines and walls of religions.

I put away the journal and took some time to observe my site one last time. I went for a walk, taking in all I could, wondering how this whole experience would affect me after the trip.

The water of the creek was ice-cold, but refreshing, as I sat down in it to wash up. I rolled up my sleeping bag and completed packing. With two of my seven gallons of water remaining, and thinking we might need them at base camp, I tied them and the empties together and hung them from my backpack. I made sure to leave the site as it was when I had arrived, returning the prayer circle rocks to their previous places. I did put one small rock from the circle in my backpack as a reminder of the experience. Finally, with a thank you to the site and a small offering of loose tobacco thrown to the wind, I began the long hike to base camp.

As I walked, I looked up to see the eagles again circling high above the edge of the canyons. I smiled, tipped my hat to them and continued walking, wondering if it would be difficult for me to re-enter the rat race of my previous life. After walking for most of an hour through the canyon, I rounded a corner to see the camp in the distance. Being the farthest distance from base camp, it appeared that I was the final participant back to camp.

As I approached, I could see that both Jack and Martin were waiting inside the rock circle for me. I stepped over the rocks. John smiled and said quietly,

"Welcome back, Will." I had no words, and didn't try for them, offering a nod, and a smile, instead. I gave each of them a hug. I wasn't sure why, but tears began to flow and I couldn't stop them. I didn't try.

"A lot happened out there, Jack," I said quietly, almost unable to get the words out.

He nodded and squeezed my arm in a knowing way. "That's why you were here, Will."

Martin walked around me, waving the smudge stick. I enjoyed the spiritual rite quietly while it unfolded. Finally, he finished the ritual and looked me in the eye and said with a caring smile,

"Welcome back, my friend. You can move out of the circle when you are ready to move back into the world we live in. As you step out, share your experience with your eyes only as you greet the others."

I stood for a few moments, not sure if I was ready to leave what I had experienced, or if ready to return to my previous world. Finally, knowing I had to, I stepped out. The other participants were circled around the rocks during the ritual. Each now stepped up and gave me a hug. I knew they, too, had gone through their own emotional and gratifying experiences. No words were shared, and none needed. With each hug, a prolonged gaze into each set of eyes said it all. They knew what I knew.

Jack said that our experiences might not make sense for some time and not to try to understand it too quickly. The experience would need time to percolate within us. He asked that we not talk about what we had gone through until we got back to the kiva the next morning. There, we would begin the process of trying to understand it all. I was fine with that. I was emotionally drained. We were welcomed back to base camp with fragrant herbal teas and sandwiches of whole-grain breads piled high with a variety of organic vegetables and cheeses. It was delicious. I hadn't eaten for five days, and had not been hungry for four! I then realized that I hadn't had even one headache from caffeine withdrawal. I wasn't sure how to explain it all, and I didn't try. I filed it away as another amazing event of many that had occurred over the five days. As I savored the delicious food, I smiled to myself realizing that I had finally found a foolproof method for breaking the caffeine habit and for losing weight. I would later find that I had lost twelve pounds over the five days.

After eating, we packed up our base camp tents and the camp kitchen and began multiple trips to the vehicles. It was a good thing that we hadn't tried to cross the creek with the vehicles. The rain had raised the water level considerably. It was above our knees and our vehicles would not have made it through. After three trips, we lashed our gear to the roof racks and began the long drive back to Santa Fe. Occupied with our own private thoughts, it was a quiet drive. After a couple of hours, we stopped at the Abiquiu Reservoir to have a much-deserved swim. Relaxed and re-energized, we loaded up for the trip back to the retreat in Santa Fe.

After a relaxing afternoon off and a long hot shower, we went to dinner at the same Mexican restaurant we had gone to before the Quest. Perhaps due to our stomachs shrinking during the Quest, none of us ate much. Exhausted, we all retired early. The plans for our final day would have us again visit the kiva to try to make sense of all we had gone through. It would also be the place where we would go our separate ways.

As tired as I felt, I found it hard to sleep that night. I was inside four walls again, and missed being in the outdoors. Trying too hard to make sense of it all, my mind would not shut down. And it was too quiet! I finally picked up my blankets and went out on the back deck to sleep. I felt the need to reconnect with nature. Even outside, it was a rough night of intermittent sleep.

In the morning, after a quick breakfast of oatmeal and herbal tea, we again drove to the kiva. We were far more prepared for our second visit, having now experienced both the kiva and the Quest. I felt the full spiritual nature of the place as we entered via the ladder. Martin was again there to help us prepare, waving the smoking smudge stick around our bodies as we entered. We once again sat around the exterior walls, facing the center of the room.

After a few quiet moments, Jack stood and spoke, "We are here to have each of you share, if you choose, about your Quest. A good place to begin is to begin by stating why you came here for this experience."

The prayer stick made its way around the room again. This time, I went last. The depth of the others' experiences awed me. All had been deeply moved by their five days alone. It was clear that everyone was trying to understand their place in this world, to find happiness and contentment, and to grow spiritually. As I shared my experience, the others nodded as I spoke about things that I knew these folks could fully understand. The dream of the final night was the last thing I talked about. I knew it struck a chord with them as they, too, had spoken of their own powerful dreams.

As we climbed out of the kiva and back into the real world, we took a picture of the group and final hugs were shared. I hitched a ride back to Jack's place to pick up my motorcycle. Before getting on the bike, I told Jack how much this experience had meant to me.

"I could tell, Will," he said. "I knew from my prayers at the base site that you were going through something very special."

I hugged him and said, "I hope to see you again down the road, my friend."

"You take care," he said. "Go back and teach what you've learned. I know you will be a better teacher and coach for having gone through this."

I nodded in agreement, a lump in my throat not allowing me to say more. I hoped he was right.

Barbara, my radio personality friend from San Francisco needed a ride to the Albuquerque airport where I was headed to pick up my daughter Deidre later in the day. I had offered her a ride at the kiva and she accepted with a big smile, saying, "I've never been on a motorcycle. Looks like lots of new experiences are happening to me."

I strapped her bag on the top of luggage rack and we rode south, stopping in the small town of Madrid for a break. A pleasant surprise, Madrid was a beautiful little village of artists and shops in the middle of nowhere. It had a very positive spiritual feel to it and I could see how people were drawn to the place. We sat for a relaxing cup of tea on the front deck of a cafe, talking about the complexities of our lives and how both of us now wanted to try to simplify things.

Our waiter brought more hot water, and I asked him if he was from Madrid. His response surprised me, "Nope. I moved here a few years ago so I could slow my life down. I spent 20 years on Wall Street, and all the craziness that went with that life. Finally, I decided that I'd had enough of it. My life here is way healthier." I could tell from his contagious smile that he spoke from the heart.

"Good for you" I said, casting a knowing glance to Barbara. She winked back.

We continued on to Albuquerque. At the airport, I said goodbye to my new friend. She reached into her backpack and pulled out a small feather she had found on her Quest. "Keep this close when you need guidance," she said with a smile.

I thanked her, hugged her and asked her if she thought the experience would make her a better radio personality.

She answered quickly with a smile, "It'll make me a better person." I smiled back as she walked away to her gate. It was my last connection with an amazing group of people and a week that I would never forget.

Deidre was still an hour away, so I had a cup of herbal tea and found a quiet seat by myself to try and process everything that had happened over the past week. I took out the journal and re-read everything I had written on the trip. Wow, I thought. What a story this is! And all of this had begun because of a meeting with a stranger in Cody, Wyoming.

An hour later, our middle child walked through the door into the arrival area, her flight from Denver right on time. I was so proud of my twelve-year-old, who was flying alone for the first time. She was carrying a large backpack and a motorcycle helmet under her arm.

With her usual endless energy, she bounded up to me with a big smile.

"Hi Dad!" I lifted her up and I gave her a bear hug.

"How was the trip?" I asked with a big smile.

"Good! I had a window seat for both flights. It was great!"

"No problems with changing flights in Denver?"

"Nope! I didn't need anyone's help at all. How was your trip?"

"Pretty special, Sweetie. I'll tell you about it later on our trip."

I wondered how I could explain to her, or anyone for that matter, what had happened to me. I had just been through something precious and part of me wanted it to stay private, at least until I could process it all. I pledged to myself to try to make the rest of this trip something very special for her. We loaded the bike with her gear and put on our helmets.

"You ready, girl?" I asked with a smile.

"Yup!" she responded, giddy with excitement. I steered the bike away from the parking lot as she tapped me on the shoulder and pointed to the right. Just outside the airport property was another Waffle House. It had just been a week since I had stopped at the Waffle House in Kansas City. It seemed like a lifetime ago.

I smiled and yelled over my shoulder, "Hungry?"

"Yes. Let's stop!"

After eating waffles, we finally hit the road and began the next segment of our trip.

At Sedona, Arizona, our destination for the night, we set up camp at a beautiful campsite and rode into town for dinner and to make reservations for a jeep ride through some of the area. The next morning, our Jeep tour guide showed us why Sedona is considered such a spiritual place. Both of us could feel the energy of the place.

Hot and dry, Kingman, Arizona was our goal for the next night and we made it early, deciding to stay in an air-conditioned room instead of camping. We took in a movie and went to bed early, anxious for the big ride that would take us to L.A. the next day. Up early, we left at six hoping to miss some of the heat of the day. The ride would take us through the Mojave Desert and by Needles, CA, often called the hottest town in America. It was. The bike registered over 114 degrees as we passed through Needles, and it didn't get any cooler most of the way to L.A. The final forty miles to Santa Monica were on crowded freeways. I was back in the rat race for sure. We finally made it into Santa Monica at around three in the afternoon and met up with our good friends Jack and Judy, who had moved from Iowa to California several years before.

We spent three great days in Los Angeles visiting museums and the beaches, even getting surfing lessons for Deidre. The best athlete of the family, she was a natural at it. I tried, when asked by our host, to explain what I had been through on the Quest. I had to tell them that it was very hard to talk about it as I had not fully processed it all myself. They understood, and didn't mention it again.

After three special days in L.A., we said goodbye to Jack and Judy and began the long ride east toward Iowa. Our first stop would be Las Vegas. We made it there by nightfall, after the hottest riding of the trip. The thermometer rose to 116 as we crossed the Mojave Desert, forcing us to drink gallons of water along the way. Unable to take the heat, we stopped midday at a gas station oasis. We stayed over an hour, just happy to be in the air conditioning. We each had two pieces of pie and ate them slowly, savoring the cool air. After countless glasses of ice water, we again hit the hot road, wondering how soon we would arrive at the next oasis.

It was 9:00pm when we finally pulled onto the Vegas strip, exhausted from the heat. I made a point to do better planning as our late departure from Santa Monica had put us in the desert in the heat of the day. It was hard riding, but with no complaints from my partner.

We found a small, clean hotel off the strip, checked in and took much-needed showers. We then hiked to the strip and had a late dinner where I talked to Deidre about the negative energy I was feeling coming from Las Vegas. It was not what I considered a family destination; it was about escape, spending money, and worse. "They call it Sin-City for a reason," I thought to myself. Having just gone through a Vision Quest experience that embraced nature and truth, I was very uncomfortable with this artificial artifice. I was happy to move on as soon as we could.

Having not gambled a cent, we left early in the morning, pointing the bike northeast toward Utah. Our relaxed travel plans would take us through Utah and the National Parks there, to the Sundance Resort outside of Provo, and finally across Colorado.

We spent four very good days in Utah and Colorado, seeing many of the most beautiful National Parks in the U.S. The bike ran perfectly, and we used a combination of small hotels and camping along the way. The only rules we used were no Interstates and no fast food. Everything else was determined day-to-day. Deidre was a perfect travel-mate, as she, too, loved the God-made sites over the man-made. It was a trip that I think both of us will always treasure. We finally made it back to Iowa, after having been away for three weeks. While it was great to be home, I was sad that it was all over. The Vision Quest experience, the most spiritual personal event I had ever experienced, along with the special trip with my daughter, was something I knew I would always cherish. I knew Deidre felt the same way about her trip. Unfortunately, the trip was over, and the rat race was calling us back.

Part Four

One More Time

Teachers not only teach, they also learn.
Sauk Indian Saying

The Vision Quest experience has had a profound effect on both how I coach and how I view life. I now try to see things from the perspective of others before my own. I have become much closer to nature; taking advantage of every chance I can to spend time in natural settings. I've actually changed some of our training venues so the runners can take advantage of natural settings for their runs. Distance running is a very spiritual thing. I believe the spiritual side of the sport is every bit as important as the physical side, and is best accessed in a God-made environment. Our runners know this truth, and treasure these venues for running.

Five years after the Vision Quest experience, our youngest daughter, Nicolette, told me it was her turn for a father-daughter trip. While I had often dreamed of a return trip to the west on the bike, she chose instead to go east to Washington, DC for her trip. While it was amazing, and a wonderful bonding time for us, it was not at all like the trips out west with the other two children. Washington, DC is the definition of a "man-made" place. With safety concerns about riding the bike in the traffic of the east, we chose, instead, to opt for our Jeep. While the enclosed cocoon of the air-conditioned jeep made the trip comfortable, it also kept us from a level of participation that the bikes had provided on the other trips. Still, it was a special time with my youngest.

We spent several days visiting museums and monuments. Nikki was happy, so I was happy. Everything about Washington, DC is big, and the size of the buildings made an impact on both of us.

"Dad, these buildings are so big!" Of course, she was right. It's a place of big money, big power, and of course, some big egos. The buildings fit the place. While I had not wanted the other trips to end, I was ready to leave DC after a few days. I missed being in nature. We found ourselves racing through our daily schedule, intent on seeing everything we could while there. There is only one speed in DC: "fast." Like everyone else, we had jumped on the hurry train. At least the evenings provided some solitude and relaxation ... we camped outside of DC for the entire visit.

I was most impressed with my youngest when she later said that her favorite part of the trip was visiting the memorials and Arlington Cemetery. We stood silent at the stark Vietnam memorial, watching family members and fellow soldiers as they found loved ones' names on the wall. I could tell she was touched by the experience. I certainly was.

When I had asked Nikki at the start of our trip what she wanted to see the most, she had said the Lincoln Memorial. When we went there, she read every word of Lincoln's on the walls. My youngest was no longer a little girl. She was old enough to understand what Lincoln had meant to this country. I had her stand on the spot where Martin Luther King had given his famous "I Have a Dream" speech from the volatile 1960's, telling her how important that day, and that speech, was to this country. It was a wonderful trip, even if we had not made it on the motorcycle.

We returned to Iowa and our normal day-to-day life and I regretted that I would not get back out to Wyoming to see Great Thunder again. It just wasn't to be. He had said it would happen again some day, and I could only hope it would.

The Call Of The West

The following spring, I found my intuitive side again speaking to me. I was getting the itch to return to Wyoming on the bike. All of the children would be busy during late July, the only time I could free up to make the trip. Our youngest would be doing a mother-daughter trip to Canada to see her Grandma. The oldest two were too busy to go. Cameron, now at the University of Iowa in Iowa City, was taking summer classes as well as working and could not get free. Deidre, also a student at Iowa, was in Ann Arbor, Michigan for the summer, working with springboard diving coach Dick Kimball. She had finished 15th at the Senior Diving Nationals in Pasadena and was quickly developing into one of America's best young divers. All three kids were busy defining their own paths.

For some time, I had known I would make one more bike trip and that I would probably make it alone. Of all the bike trips, this one had the firmest direction and goal. I was making the trip to see Great Thunder and to continue writing the special story of what had happened to me on the previous ventures. I was hopeful of more discussions and perhaps another personal spiritual experience. I had no address or phone number for Great Thunder, but I felt sure I could find him. If not at his cabin, I knew someone at the Irma Hotel in Cody could probably help me locate him.

The trip out was interesting. I rode the BMW only on two-lane highways across Iowa and Nebraska, finally turning north to get to the Black Hills. I was two weeks ahead of the big Sturgis Harley Rally in the area and was glad for it. Riding through the Black Hills was a treat, as it was perfect cycling weather on beautiful roads. I was glad I didn't have to share those roads with a hundred thousand other cyclists soon to be in the area. I missed Rushmore this time, wanting to avoid the crowds, but I did make it by the Crazy Horse Memorial, where I pulled over and spent a few respectful minutes in honor of the great warrior. Then it was a short drive west to Devils Tower, a significant national monument and one of great spiritual value to Native Americans. At over 1260 feet above its base, the giant volcanic monolith can be seen for many miles away. The Natives call it Mato Tipila, meaning Bear Lodge.

I pulled up into the parking lot of a small café at the base of the Tower. I noticed that a number of other BMW bikes were parked in the lot. As I stood in line for a cup of tea, I asked one of the men where they were headed.

He responded,

"The big National BMW Bike Rally is in Gillette, Wyoming this weekend. We're all headed out there."

I wished him safe travels and walked out on the big deck that looked up to the monument. I couldn't help but overhear the small talk of an increasingly large BMW biker group. Most of the talk centered on their cycles and their jobs. It was an interesting crowd. I guessed that many of these men had high-paying white-collar jobs and this trip was providing a needed release from the 9-5 life for a few days.

Devils Tower is a very special spiritual site to Native Americans, yet I heard none of the men speaking about the place itself. We were sitting at the base of one of the greatest natural monuments in the country, and it was not a part of the conversation. Perhaps it was another indication that it is hard for us to slow down enough to appreciate the things around us that are really meaningful. I could certainly understand that ... I had been on that same treadmill for years.

After finishing my tea, I mounted up and continued on to Gillette, deciding to make a quick stop to see what the big BMW Bike Rally was all about. I only stayed an hour -- there were far too many people and motorcycles for me. It wasn't what I was looking for on this trip, so I quickly headed back out on the road. Twenty miles out of Gillette, the yellow low-fuel light came on. I knew I had less than a gallon at the most and I didn't want to run out of fuel this far out into the middle of Wyoming. I thought about turning back for Gillette, but seeing a sign that said "next gas ten miles," decided to forge ahead. I made the miles easily and pulled off the exit to see only a small café with one pump. On the pump was a hand-written sign, "No gas today."

Great! I thought. I was still twenty-five miles from Sheridan. I wasn't sure I could make it, but it was probably equally far back to Gillette: so, I decided to forge ahead, slowing down to save fuel.

I made it fifteen miles when the engine began sputtering. I pulled over, smiling and thinking to myself,

Well, you've done it now, Boy Scout! Ten miles from nowhere and not another vehicle in sight.

I looked around. It was too far to walk. `I pulled out my phone, hoping I had coverage and called information in Sheridan. I was quickly patched through to a truck stop in Sheridan. Ten miles away, they said they would send a truck out with a can of gas. Thankful for my good fortune, I pulled the bike as far off the highway as I could and took a good look around. It was an endless land devoid of trees; no doubt this was Native American country just 150 years ago. I wondered how much it had changed over those years. As far as I could see, there was no indication of civilization, just this lonely strip of asphalt running through it.

Twenty minutes later a beat-up 1960's-vintage pickup arrived with an older gentleman behind the wheel.

"Looks like you could use this," he said with a big smile as he got out of the truck holding a one-gallon gas can.

"Yes Sir! You just saved my ass!" I responded with a smile. I paid him for the gas and asked how much I needed to give him for the trouble.

"Oh, nothing. Maybe if you stop by our place and fill up in Sheridan, that will take care of it."

I thanked him and said,

"You went to some trouble and expense to come the ten miles out here." I finished emptying the small can and gave him another thirty dollars and said, "You're a good man, and I should have been paying attention to my gas."

"Lots of bikers go through here – good people," he said.

I thanked him again and said I would stop at his place to fill up the tank. I told him to lead the way and we were off to Sheridan.

After gassing up at the truck stop and having a candy bar and iced tea, I turned the bike directly west and headed for Cody. I knew I would make it before dark. I was excited about the prospect of seeing my old friend again. As I drove across Wyoming on Hwy 14, I crossed through the Bighorn Mountains. It was a beautiful climb and I stopped near the summit to watch a number of hang gliders take off, flying down to Sheridan. It was a pretty site and I wondered what the eagles in the area thought of these strange oversized birds with their thermal-flying ability.

After the last hang glider took off, I mounted up and continued west. Great Thunder's letter came to mind as I climbed toward the pass. Having long ago memorized its contents, I thought about what he had written on wisdom:

Seek wisdom, not knowledge. Books can give us knowledge of the past. Only life experiences can give us wisdom. Wisdom is about the future, not the past. You have the potential for great wisdom, but you must first live more of life's experiences.

I had continued to read and grow intellectually after my initial meeting with Great Thunder, but the Vision Quest experience had imprinted on me the need to apply my knowledge with wisdom. I made every effort to fully live experiences since the Quest. I also made sure that the athletes were taking more ownership of their program (when they were ready).

I rode into Cody as the sun set. I found the same small motel off the main drag that Cameron and I had stayed at years ago and pulled the bike in.

"You look tired, young man," smiled the middle-aged lady at the desk. "I've got just the room for you."

"I bet you do," I said with my own smile, "Probably a room with a great view?"

"They all have that," she said with a laugh, "A view of the parking lot or the main drag."

I laughed with her and asked, "Anything quiet?"

"I can put you all the way back from the road," she said. "It's pretty quiet back there. How many nights?"

I hadn't thought about that.

"How about one, to start. I may stay longer, but I'll let you know."

I unloaded my gear into a small, but clean non-smoking room. I took the bike across the street to the car wash I had used on the trip with Cameron. After my own shower, I walked down the main drag to the Irma Hotel for a bite to eat, hoping I might get lucky and run into Great Thunder. I needed the exercise, and was tired from sitting on the saddle all day.

I entered the historic place and saw that all of the stools at the bar were full, so I was given a small two-place table at the window. I had a quick look around the place hoping to see my wise friend. No luck. I ordered soup and salad and asked for a pitcher of water as I realized how dehydrated I was from the ride.

When the waitress returned with the food, I asked if she knew of a Native American gentleman by the name of Great Thunder who ate here on occasion. She did not, but said she would ask some others in back if they might know. I ate the soup and salad quickly, realizing how hungry I was after a long day on the bike. When the waitress came back, she asked if I wanted dessert or coffee. I said coffee only. As she was walking off, she looked back over her shoulder, saying,

"One of the guys out back knows the person you were asking about. He'll be out in a minute to talk with you."

"Thanks!" I said, as she disappeared through some swinging doors, already out of earshot.

Now excited, I savored a surprisingly good cup of coffee. Maybe I would get to see him again! I thought more about what Great Thunder had written in his letter:

You shape your own spirit with the choices you make every day. When we make choices that are wrong, we will ultimately have to pay for those.

God knows that I've made my share of mistakes and bad choices in my life. Selfishness, a need to prove myself to others, and a lack of respect for others had been behind most of those mistakes. There was no doubt in my mind there would be a price to pay for those bad choices — God knows, I'd already paid for some of them. I also felt that I could, hopefully, nullify some of those mistakes with right actions now. I couldn't take those mistakes back, but I could grow from them. I smiled to myself: I might be on a long repayment schedule."

"Sir, you were asking about Great Thunder?" I was jarred from my thoughts by a young man of about twenty-five in a cook's apron.

"Yes! Yes! Do you know him?" I asked.

"Yes, I do. He comes in here a couple of times a week for lunch. He might be here tomorrow. Do you want me to leave him a message?"

"Yes, please," I said. "If he comes in before lunch tomorrow, please tell him an old friend will stop by at lunch tomorrow. I've come a long way to see him. Thanks very much!"

"You're welcome, sir. Can we get you anything else?"

"No, I'm good. Thanks again." I replied.

"My pleasure, sir. Are you going out to the rodeo tonight?"

"You know, I think I will make it to the Rodeo tonight." The bill was for just over $11.00 and I left a good tip, appreciative of the information about Great Thunder.

As I walked back to the motel, I again thought about Great Thunder's letter:

Find time for solitude, to think without outside interference. This will be important to you. It will require you to get over the fear of being alone. This fear is something all people feel. Only the strongest have learned how to be alone and to enjoy what solitude can offer. It is necessary for us to grow spiritually.

Like the Vision Quest, this trip was also about being alone. I was no longer afraid of solitude as I was before the Quest. That second bike trip had been about me facing my fear of being alone and taught me to face issues head on and deal with them.

I was happy to be back in this environment. I rode the bike to the west side of town to the Rodeo grounds. The large entrance sign indicated the show would start at 8:00 -- like every other night in the summer. I pulled into the big parking lot and made my way to the ticket window.

As I sat in the stands and watched the preparations for the big show, I thought about what this particular trip might mean to me: more talks with Great Thunder and time to be alone on the bike. I wasn't sure where I would point the bike after Cody; I just felt good about being here again. I thought about sitting in these stands with Cameron so many years before. It seemed like such a long time ago. I was a different person then, smart about some things yet needing serious work on other things. I hoped I would get to see Great Thunder again. I wondered what he would have to say this time around. I was anxious to tell him about the Vision Quest and all the things that had happened since we had seen each other so many years ago.

The rodeo that night was entertaining but secondary to my thoughts as I sat in the stands with my mind miles away. So much had happened after that first trip here with Cameron ... and here I was again in Cody. I'd come full circle over the ten years. Finally, unable to focus on the rodeo, I decided to leave early. With my mind full of thoughts, I was anxious to get back to the hotel room and write in my journal. I walked to the bike, put my helmet on, and stepped over the seat. Just as I was ready to turn the key, a horn honked behind me. I looked over my shoulder and into the bright lights of what looked like a pickup truck pulling up beside me.

A man looked out, saying, "I wondered how long it would take you to get back up this way, Coach."
"My God! It was Great Thunder!

A Friendship Renewed

I laughed and stuck out my hand. He reached out of the cab window and shook my hand, saying

"I got a call from a friend at the Irma. He said you might be here tonight. I had a feeling it was probably you. I've been expecting you for some time now."

"I'm no longer surprised at that sort of thing," I said, still smiling. "A lot has happened since we last talked. How about some herbal tea or coffee? I've got lots to tell you."

"I know just the place," he said. "Follow me."

We drove into town and turned off the main drag to a side street where there was a small coffee shop. Sitting at the Café's only outdoor table, we had a quiet private place to talk.

"You look pretty good, Coach."

"You, too," I said. "So you knew I was coming out?"

"Yes," he answered, "I've known for a while. How many years since we last talked?"

"Too many," I said. "A lot has happened since that first trip here."

"I expect so, Coach. I knew when you were here before that you had much to experience. And it's not over, yet. You know that, right?" I nodded, as a waitress appeared to take our orders. We both ordered decaffeinated coffee and Great Thunder asked what had happened since my first visit to Cody.

"It's a long story ... but a good one," I said with a smile.

I told him about how I had gone back to Grinnell after the first trip to Cody and had basically fallen back into the same day-to-day routine. I explained how I had been told in a dream, while on a sabbatical leave, to do the Quest ... and where I would do it. He nodded and listened intently. I went through the whole Vision Quest experience and how it had impacted me, especially the dream I'd had on the final night.

He continued to nod, and asked,

"Has the Vision Quest experience positively impacted how you teach and deal with other people?"

"Absolutely," I said. "I just feel differently about a lot of things ... especially when it comes to understanding what really matters. I should also tell you that I have become fascinated by nature. I love being in natural environments, and try to make that happen every chance I can."

"That's common to those who have a strong Vision Quest experience," he said. "How's your boy Cameron doing?"

"He's doing great, now," I said. "It was rough there for a while. We thought he was going down a path that was not the best, but we had to let him go there. He was an excellent student, but was totally non-motivated to do school work. He just didn't want to jump through the hoops. It was hard for a while because he said he wasn't interested in preparing for college. We finally backed off and let him go his own path."

"What made you decide to do that?" he asked with real interest.

"Our pushing him to do what we wanted was only pushing him further away from us. We finally realized that he needed to find his own path. Seems like it had to be a bit rockier than it should have been ... but it had to be his path and not ours."

"Exactly, Coach. All of us have a path, and it needs to be our own. We all must take possession of our lives. When others try to do it for us, it creates tension that can manifest in a lot of ways, most of them bad. I expect your boy was fighting to take possession. I also expect he has done some growing in the process since."

"Yes, he has." I replied. "We're mighty proud of him. He's now in college, of his own choice ... and doing great there. He has a direction now ... he's thinking psychology."

"That's great news, Coach!" he replied with a genuine smile.

As our coffee cups were refilled, Great Thunder said,

"There is no doubt that you had a powerful experience while out on your Quest. But all of us who have had a powerful Vision Quest must also return home afterward. We come home to the same challenges and problems we had before we left. The difference is that we have more wisdom to help us to handle things. The challenge is to not fall back into the same lifestyle. The blunt truth is that we cannot find happiness and contentment from the man-made things that we come back to. Money and fame ... it's all a facade. The isolation and solitude you experienced while on the Quest is what you needed to be able to reflect on the things that really matter."

"I agree," I said. "I try to make time for those things that matter: family, my team, nature, and solitude. I find myself thinking a lot about those things."

"Coach, I believe you have changed because of the path you have taken. It seems like you're more comfortable with yourself now."

I nodded. "Yes, I am. Before the trips, I had trouble being content, even being alone. Seems like I was always chasing something, but never really knowing what it was."

"We've all felt that way, Coach. The world has a way of pulling us along on the chase, a chase we don't even realize we are on. And the longer we stay on that path, the harder it is to get off it."

There was silence for a few moments and he asked,

"Coach, what is the greatest gift you have found on these trips?"

I thought for a few seconds, "Beyond my kids?" I asked.
He nodded.

"Well, the dream I had on the final night of the Quest was an eye-opener. I learned that all things are connected in some way; all people, all animals and everything natural on the earth. You know, I've thought a lot about this. I've learned that I feel better when I do something good ... something for another person, an animal, or the earth. Just the simple act of picking up litter can make me feel good. All of it matters, no matter how small."

"Very good, Coach," Great Thunder said with a nod of appreciation. "We all have to work to make things better. Doing something good is one way. I know I feel better about myself when I do what I believe is right."

"I have a question for you," I said. "I think spirituality is about more than religion. How do we teach spirituality?"

"I think you're doing it, Coach," he said quietly. "We teach by example. We teach people to think about what matters ... and to act on those thoughts. You know as well as I that this earth is in trouble. We are overpopulating it, we're killing it with pollution, and we're living lives driven by greed and desire."

"Yes," I said. "I've been there. I used to think that education was the key to getting things right. Now I'm not so sure that education alone can get us to where we need to go. It seems like we are stuck in terms of our spiritual development. Why can't we move forward spiritually, I mean, to include religion, but also to move beyond the walls of religion?"

Great Thunder took a drink of his coffee and said,

"People have to be ready for it. There is no doubt that religion has its place in spiritual development. Unfortunately, many folks live religious spirituality only on Sundays. There's a lack of integrity in living a week of bad choices, then trying to make up for it on Sunday. I, too, believe religion has its place, but historically it has also been the root of many wars. There are many paths to spirituality. Religion is a good one, but it is only one path."

"You know," I said, "In the letter that you left me on my first trip here, you said that I had to find harmony with nature ... for my own spiritual development. I believe this. The time on my Vision Quest showed me that. The connection with that place and the animals ... it was intense."

"Yes, intensity and feelings you likely would not have felt had you not first peeled away the layers of the man-made life covering you. You know, Coach, we all have the potential to find our inner selves. Most don't try, or won't try. A lot of people are happy living life from the outside in. I expect this will be your challenge from this point on, to teach those around you about this. Our children will face issues and challenges far greater than those we have faced. The answers to those problems will have to come from their hearts and souls, and not just from their minds. Spiritual development is the key. People must be open to the various paths to spiritual development. Unfortunately, people are often not open to thinking about other ways of looking at the world. We get locked into dogmas, unable to open up to other ways of seeing things."

"I know. It's a big challenge. I'm not sure how much of an effect I can have," I said.

"You can have a big effect, Coach. I know this. You have already fought the norm when it comes to your coaching. You are not afraid to do things differently. What you're doing is making a difference."

"Yes, but it's not always been an easy path," I responded. "Sport is about competition ... and competition is not always the smoothest path to spiritual growth."

We spent another hour talking. I was certain now that I had been led to meet this man. Incredibly intelligent and wise, he also showed a level of contentment, compassion and spirituality that was extraordinary to me. After a second cup of coffee, he said,

"Do you remember when I gave you some great apple pie at my cabin?"

"Yes, it was incredible pie," I said, smiling at the memory.

"That lady I told you about that made it? We got married last year."

"Well, congratulations!" I smiled, reaching out to shake his hand. "That's great news!"

"We have to drive down to Arizona in the morning for a wedding. That's why I came out to find you at the rodeo tonight. I wanted to make sure we got together before I had to leave."

"I appreciate that, Great Thunder. I really do. The primary purpose of this trip was to meet up again. I had a gut feeling that we would cross paths."

"Listen," he said, "How about you come up to the cabin tomorrow and spend a couple of days there. It will be good for you to get away and have some time to think. No charge for the room. The key is still under the same rock out back. There is plenty of food and you won't be bothered by anyone." He paused and then with a smile, said, "I think you should do this, Coach."

I thought for a few seconds, asking, "You sure about this?"

"Consider it another chapter to your search," he replied. After a few moments of silence, he added, "I need to go now. We have to leave before sun up. Do come up, Coach. It will be good for you."

One More Time

I said I would be up by mid-morning. Feeling a bit sad, I extended my hand again and said, "I can't thank you enough for helping me. I'm a different person for having gone through all of this. You're a big reason for what has happened to me."

Great Thunder continued the handshake and grabbed my arm with his other hand, and said,

"My job is to help others. And so is yours. You're making a big difference, Coach. Keep it up. What you're doing matters."

With a final gaze into my eyes, he went on,

"Continue to listen to your dreams. They will tell you plenty. Listen also to your heart to make the choices that are right. It is not a whole lot more difficult than that. Your best days are ahead."

"You sound pretty sure of that," I said with a skeptical smile.

He got into his truck and looked out the open window.

"Coach, I think you get it. Your job is to help others to get it. There is plenty for all to learn. Your best day will be always be your next day. I'll put a white bandana on a post by the turn off, just in case you've forgotten the way." He hesitated for a moment and then, looking in my eyes, said, "Stay the path, Coach." With that, and a wave, he was gone.

I waved back and sat down, thinking, "Well, I got to see him again, as I knew I would -- even if only for a couple of hours."

As usual, talking with him had my head spinning. Maybe someday I will have his level of commitment to help others. I finished my coffee, now cold, and mounted the bike to ride back to the hotel. I told the lady at the desk that I would be checking out in the morning.

"Didn't like the room?" she asked.

"Oh, no, the room was great," I said, "I'll be moving on, that's all." I slept hard that night, comfortable that I had accomplished what I needed to do on the trip, to see Great Thunder once more.

In the morning, I packed the bike and stopped at a small local breakfast spot on the main drag. I sat outside at a small table on the sidewalk and had coffee and a pastry. After breakfast, I visited some of the shops on the main drag, finding a small gift to leave at Great Thunder's cabin. Traffic was picking up as cars heading west to Yellowstone Park began to clog the main drag. Maybe I did need a couple days on the mountain.

The drive up to the cabin was as beautiful as I had remembered, with spectacular vistas all the way up the many switchbacks. This time, a large group of bicyclists were making the Climb up the Chief Joseph Highway. I pulled off at one of the overlooks to admire the view. I recalled once reading that many considered this the prettiest motorcycle ride in North America. From this vantage point, it was hard to disagree.

I spotted the bandana on the post and pulled over to grab it. Then, it was up the long gravel road, the destination still several miles ahead. Finally, I pulled up to the cabin and parked the bike, surveying the view. "Just like before," I thought. "Still the most amazing cabin and the most beautiful view."

As expected, I found the key under the white rock, and I took my bags inside. As I sat them down, I noticed an envelope on the table with "Coach" written on it. I took it outside and sat on the porch step and opened it.

Dear Coach,

It was really good to see you again. I wish I could be here longer, but I must honor my commitment to this wedding. I can tell that your journey, since we last met, has held fear, surprise and joy ... and most of all, recognition of the things that matter most in life. The path we take is one that will have it all ... good and bad. It is our job to make sense of, and learn from, all of it.

Coach, you came to me for a reason many years ago. It is good that you have listened to your intuitive side and followed through on the Vision Quest. I can tell that it was very good for your spiritual growth. I believe my job is done with you. Your job, however, is not done. You have been given a gift to teach others. I believe that your approach to athletics is a healthy and beneficial one to those you coach. There is no doubt that teaching is a calling for you. I offer you these thoughts as you go forward:

-Keep your family close. Family ties are like no other, and family members can help each other like no other can, especially in hard times.
-Competition is a good thing when done in a healthy manner. Competition is a test for us. It moves us out of the comfort zone of everyday life. This is how we grow. But competition can also be a debilitating, negative thing if handled poorly. Competition is ultimately about achievement, not beating another. Continue to find a way to make competition work for the athlete. Competition with integrity is the goal.
-Continue to listen to your intuitive side. I believe you have a gift for this. It can be of great help to you, both as a parent and coach. Do not be afraid to act when intuition speaks to you. Know that your dreams are part of intuition. Reflect on them, they will tell you plenty.
-Self-acceptance is one of the hardest challenges we face. It requires that we think from the inside-out and not from the outside-in. Life will

control us, and define us, if we let it. Choose to take control, and to accept your essence. You do have a choice!

-Know that all people and all things in nature are connected to each other. You learned this on your Quest.

-Give before taking. You know that you feel better when you give to, or help, another. Likewise, we feel better when we do something positive for Mother Earth. Whether giving to people or the Earth, giving means to give positive energy. Taking means we take energy from others (or the earth). You know the difference. Choose to give.

-Listen to, and respect, the earth and all life upon it. We only have one earth ... and we are not doing well with it. It talks to us, if only we listen. You know this now.

-Follow your heart. Think with your mind and heart. Your knowledge is great, but wisdom does not come so easy. You have gained much wisdom since our first meeting. Every experience will bring more wisdom.

You no longer need my help, Coach. I have given you what I can. Now it is up to you. You no longer have to prove yourself to another. You are successful because you have chosen to do things differently, and you believe in those methods passionately. It is now your job to teach others the things you have learned. Teach them with stories and by action. Trust in your skills and stay the path! You are making a difference. Meeting you was my pleasure.

Respectfully,
Great Thunder

I folded the letter, and looked up at the beautiful view, unable to contain my tears.

Afterward

If he is indeed wise, he does not bid you enter the house of wisdom, but rather leads you to the threshold of your mind.
Kahlil Gibran

This amazing story happened to me over a period of ten years and three very special motorcycle trips across the country, two with my children and one alone. The original motivation was to take each of my kids on a special father-child trip on a motorcycle, a chance for us to really see the country in a way that we couldn't in a car. These wonderful bonding trips with my children also became part of a very special personal spiritual journey.

Both Cameron and Deidre made great travel partners on the bikes (as did Nicolette, although her trip was to the east and not on a bike). All three are older now, and on their own paths. All three attend the University of Iowa: Cameron is studying Psychology, Deidre graduated with degrees in Religious Studies and Spanish; and Nicolette is studying Communications. Deidre is the current U.S. National Champion in springboard diving, and is training full time with hopes of making the 2016 Olympic team. My wife continues to be an amazing woman. While she did not have a direct part in the story you just read, it does not diminish the incredible role she has played in our family and in my life. The two of us are planning our own special trip.

I've always felt that there is far more to life than science can explain. The emphasis of my Masters work was in biomechanics, a very quantitative field. As I began to ask questions that the scientific method could not answer, I moved into the more qualitative study of human behavior and performance. I continue to have questions every day. I'd like to say I have a lot of answers, but I don't ... at least not for others. It is up to others to ask their own questions, and to search for their own answers. I have learned a lot about myself on my path, mostly that I am more spiritual than I had previously thought. I am convinced that if we are to make a difference, we all need to awaken our spiritual sides.

I've been fortunate in my life to meet a number of people who have helped me to understand the big picture of my time on this earth. I thank and honor all of them, especially Great Thunder. This special man really did know that I was coming his way! My journey did not end with the last bike trip. It continues today ... as all of our journeys do.

I've learned a few things along the way:

I've learned that there are many ways to God ... and that God is everywhere and in everything. Everyone and everything is related and linked at a spiritual level.

I've learned to respect and be thankful for all animals and our natural environment.

I've learned to listen to my intuitive side. Intuition speaks to us more than we know. I've learned to heed its call.

I've learned that the art of coaching is at least as important as the science of coaching. It is the things outside the X's and O's that shape people the most.

I've learned that teachers must show the way, lead the way, and then know when to get out of the way. The greatest gift of a mentor is to mentor the student from dependence to independence.

I've learned that *The Way* is to give, not take. It has been the hardest thing to learn for me. Our selfish tendencies are deep-seated and difficult to break.

I've learned that we must have balance and harmony in our lives to be content, healthy and productive. It is a simple truth that we violate every day. I've been more guilty than most.

I've learned that living a life of integrity is the greatest gift to those we touch.

Finally, I have learned that we are all teachers.

After the last trip, I spent a lot of time thinking about my life's mission. I sat down and wrote the following on an index card. I carry that card in my wallet to this day as a reminder of what is important. It has only seven lines, but they pretty well say it all:

FAMILY BEFORE WORK
TEAM BEFORE ME
PROCESS BEFORE RESULT
KEEP LEARNING
KEEP PRAYING
AIM FOR QUALITY
LIVE WITH INTEGRITY

I know that if I can my live according to these seven precepts, I will be content and hopefully make a difference to others.

The big BMW bike is no longer around. I sold it after the last bike trip. Today, I cruise around on a Vespa scooter. It's more than enough bike for my day-to-day needs. As I write this, I am in Vero Beach, Florida on another sabbatical leave, finally getting this special story on paper. I found a wonderful place to write, the McKee Botanical Gardens. It has helped to be in such a beautiful, natural environment to write. I have not forgotten what Great Thunder told me. I carry some loose tobacco to spread each day around my outdoor writing table, an offering to the Great Spirit and to those who were part of the story. I hope God is pleased with the result.

The Vespa is my sole transportation here. When I ride it, I re-live the memories of those wonderful trips on the big bikes. Life has slowed down a bit ... I finally feel that I am living it at its own speed. Truth is ... I kind of like it that way.

WAF

Acknowledgements

I am grateful to many people. First, I offer my deepest appreciation and love to my wife, Evelyn, and my children, Cameron, Deidre and Nicolette. They complete my life.

A sincere thank you goes out to those who read the manuscript and offered constructive comments: Sue Montgomery, Dr. George Drake, Drake Ballew, John Kissane, John Canady, Janet Carl, Emily and John Pfitsch, Dr. Joe Vigil, Charles Salzberg, Kathrin Seitz, Dr. Idelle Cooper and Bill Downing.

I mentioned some of them in the book, but feel that I should repeat my deepest thanks to the mentors, friends and coaches who shaped my life and influenced my philosophy of life, coaching and teaching:

-Nolen and Daisy Freeman (my parents).

-Nolen Freeman, Tony Freeman, Joey Freeman, and Eric Freeman (my brothers)

-Dick Burton, Harold Barnett, Jimmy Carnes, Walter Welsch, Andy Higgins, Arthur Lydiard, Joe Vigil, Jack Daniels, and Dan Pfaff (coaches and mentors)

-Mike Cotton and Dave Roberts (my training partners and closest friends from my pole vaulting days)

-John Pfitsch (the man who hired me at Grinnell College)
-Jack Mathews and his wife Judy (who loaned me their cabin in Vero Beach to write the manuscript).

This book was a personal quest, one that could not have occurred without two very special people leading me through it. Part of the story was about a Vision Quest experience that I was called to in New Mexico.

John Wallace (Jack, in the story) led me through one of the most profound experiences in my life. I made contact with John about five years ago (four years after the Quest), telling him that I was thinking of writing about my special journey. He was totally supportive. I tried to make contact again after finishing the manuscript, and was saddened to find out that John had passed away of cancer. His passing made me appreciate even more that special week I spent in New Mexico under his guidance. I'm a better person for having crossed paths with him.

Finally, my deepest appreciation and thanks go out to Great Thunder. This gifted man offered to mentor me, asking nothing in return except that I share what I learned with others. He did ask that I honor his privacy, and I have. I can only hope that all people have the chance to encounter an extraordinary mentor like Great Thunder. To him, I can only say, "The lessons were powerful. I'm honored to have met you. Thank you, my friend."

WAF

Will Freeman

As an athlete, Will Freeman attended the University of Florida where he competed as a top pole-vaulter in the mid 1970's. The 1973 U.S. Junior Champion in the event, he later won five Southeastern Conference titles in the event (three indoor and two outdoor). An NCAA Div. I All-American, he was a finalist at the U.S. Olympic Trials. He is a member of the University of Florida Athletic Hall of Fame.

As a coach, Will Freeman has led the Grinnell College Pioneers (Grinnell, Iowa) to twenty-nine Midwest Conference titles in Cross Country and Track & Field in his thirty-three years at Grinnell. He has coached beginners to national champions while at Grinnell and has trained coaches and athletes throughout the US, in Canada, the Bahamas, and Africa. The former National Chairman for Coaching Education for the USA Track & Field, he holds Level III certification as a coach (the highest level of certification in the U.S.).

A sought-after speaker throughout the U.S. and internationally, he has also written four books, many articles and has written and performed nineteen training videos for coaches of all levels. Besides his duties as cross country and track coach, Freeman is an Associate Professor at Grinnell College and teaches popular courses in the Foundations of Sports Psychology and Sport Sociology. Freeman's wife Evelyn is the highly successful women's cross country and track coach at Grinnell. He and his wife have three children: Cameron 27, Deidre, 25 and Nicolette, 21.

www.coachwillfreeman.com

Made in the USA
Charleston, SC
09 March 2015